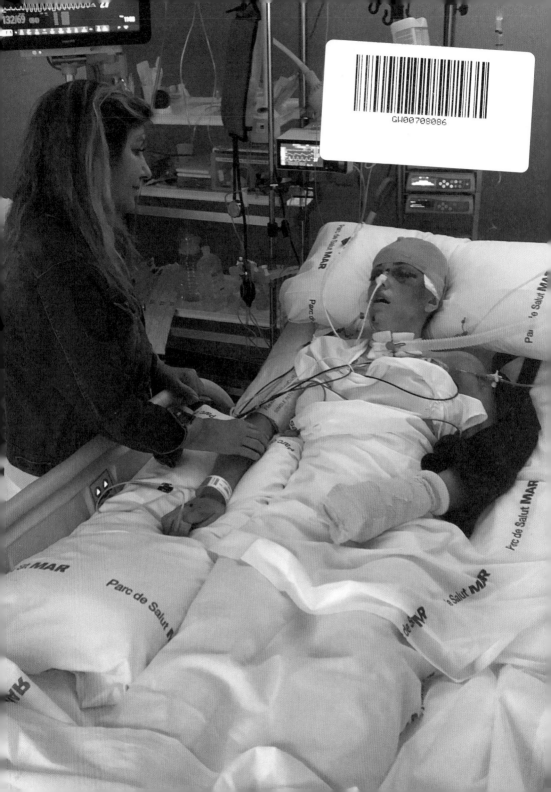

Praise for *Broken Girl*

'A love story becomes a horror story in a split second on a bright morning in Barcelona. Harrowing, yet ultimately hopeful, *Broken Girl* offers revelatory insights into the nature of traumatic brain injury and the courage – both physical and emotional – needed to fight for a full recovery.'
– Geraldine Brooks, winner of the Pulitzer Prize

'I was captivated by *Broken Girl* from start to finish. Told with flair and grace, Caroline's heartrending story of a dazzling woman struck down in her prime is a testament to the indomitable strength of the human spirit.'
– Lang Leav, international bestselling author
of *Others Were Emeralds*

'A beautiful, dark gem told with devastating honesty. I couldn't put it down. Caroline's story is a luminous account of human fragility. If you are a lover, friend, carer, health professional, or simply someone who needs reminding about the gift of your life, read *Broken Girl* today.'
– Heather Rose, author of *Nothing Bad Ever Happens Here* and *The Museum of Modern Love*

BROKEN GIRL

Also by Bradley Trevor Greive

Penguin Bloom – The Odd Little Bird Who Saved a Family

Sam Bloom – Heartache & Birdsong

The Blue Day Book

A Teaspoon of Courage

Why Dogs Are Better Than Cats

The World Is Great, and I Am Small

Priceless: The Vanishing Beauty of a Fragile Planet

In Praise of Idleness: A Timeless Essay by Bertrand Russell

A
TRUE
STORY

BROKEN GIRL

BESTSELLING AUTHOR OF *PENGUIN BLOOM*

BRADLEY TREVOR GREIVE
AND CAROLINE LANER BREURE

hachette
AUSTRALIA

Pseudonyms and composite characters have been used in this book and other details altered where necessary to protect the identity and privacy of people mentioned.

 hachette AUSTRALIA

Published in Australia and New Zealand in 2024
by Hachette Australia
(an imprint of Hachette Australia Pty Limited)
Gadigal Country, Level 17, 207 Kent Street, Sydney, NSW 2000
www.hachette.com.au

Hachette Australia acknowledges and pays our respects to the past, present and future Traditional Owners and Custodians of Country throughout Australia and recognises the continuation of cultural, spiritual and educational practices of Aboriginal and Torres Strait Islander peoples. Our head office is located on the lands of the Gadigal people of the Eora Nation.

 A catalogue record for this work is available from the National Library of Australia

ISBN: 978 0 7336 5061 1 (hardback)

Cover design and illustration by Louisa Maggio
Excerpt from 'What the Living Do', from *What the Living Do* by Marie Howe
copyright © 1997 Marie Howe. Used by permission of W. W. Norton & Company, Inc.
Roses
Words and Music by Andrew Taggart and Elizabeth Mencel
Copyright © 2015 Hipgnosis Side A, LizzleSizzle and HiFi Music IP Issuer, L.P.
All Rights on behalf of Hipgnosis Side A Administered by Hipgnosis Worldwide
All Rights on behalf of LizzleSizzle and HiFi Music IP Issuer, L.P. Administered by Songs of Kobalt Music Publishing
All Rights Reserved Used by Permission
Reprinted by Permission of Hal Leonard LLC
Typeset in Baskerville Regular, Century Gothic Regular, Goudy Old Style MT Std by Kirby Jones
Printed and bound in Australia by McPherson's Printing Group

 MIX
Paper | Supporting responsible forestry
FSC® C001695
www.fsc.org

The paper this book is printed on is certified against the Forest Stewardship Council® Standards. McPherson's Printing Group holds FSC® chain of custody certification SA-COC-005379. FSC® promotes environmentally responsible, socially beneficial and economically viable management of the world's forests.

For Juceli
Bravest mother
Truest friend

But there are moments, walking, when I catch a glimpse of
myself in the window glass,
say, the window of the corner video store, and I'm gripped by a
cherishing so deep

for my own blowing hair, chapped face, and unbuttoned coat
that I'm speechless:
I am living. I remember you.

Excerpt from *What the Living Do*
by Marie Howe

Personal disclaimer

I am telling the truth as I know it.
Imperfect, incomplete.

Some memories have been misplaced or altered by a mind
rebelling against order.

Others scream in reawakening, drowning out the details, fraying
the delicate threads of time and place that bind stars and stories
in alignment.

I have at times relied upon the recollections of others.
Those closest to me who observed my pain intimately.
Some who stayed, some who left.

Where all is shadows and echoes, I have trusted my heart to
guide me.

The names of those who wounded me deeply have been changed
for the sake of decency and kindness.
Not absolution.

Faces fade, mouths merge, even as their cruel words and crueller
silence bite into the flesh of my memory.
Scars upon scars upon scars.

Nevertheless, I am telling the truth.

May it free us both.

Prologue

I am my own mystery.

Nothing is as it seems.
Not anymore.

I know I'm broken.

Don't weep for who I was.
My mother shed enough tears for all of us.

I was stolen from her, yet I never left.
I am her daughter still.
The same girl, same woman.
Forever changed.

Perfectly imperfect.

My story is not about what was lost, but what was found.
What matters most is that which remains.

I have forgotten so much.
But I have not forgotten how to love.
So that's where I'll begin.

Sift through my pieces. Please.
Seek out the best of me.
This is my gift to you.

Accept the hope I hold dear, the dreams half-formed.

Channel my rage into your forge.
Burn brighter.

Make something beautiful for yourself from my fleeting
reminiscence.

The sunshine and laughter.
Moments of ecstasy.
Precious tears.

If these are not mine to give, then there is nothing left of me.

20.

I was born in Campo Grande, Brazil, and grew up in Caxias do Sul, my mother's sleepy hometown.
It snowed there once when I was seven.

Snowflakes falling in the rainforest.

My mother taught me that intelligence was sexy, being independent was powerful, optimism and kindness were as essential as clean water, and, above all, to trust my heart.

My father taught me not to trust men.

At seventeen I left home to attend university in Porto Alegre.
A joyful and treacherous city overlooking the swollen Guaíba River.
For better and for worse, everything that is exciting happens here.

Porto Alegre.
Hotbed of artists, musicians, writers and intellectuals.
Home to avant-garde theatre, epic book fairs, rebellions and ghost stories.
Bowlegged cowboys walk the streets, their ponchos smelling of leather and grass.
Chaotic host city to military coups, *Carnaval*, and, of course, crime.

This is Brazil, after all.
Some countries choose safety.
We choose samba.

I was robbed at gunpoint more than once.
But I also gave my virginity to Porto Alegre. Gladly.

I will always love this place.

I may be the only Brazilian who doesn't dance.
But I adore parties. Always have.
Dark strawberry cake and champagne.
Standing at the edge of the dancefloor.
Adrift in the happy swirl of laughter and lights.

When I was young my true passions were foreign languages and
mathematics; the mother tongue of the visible universe.
I was proud to be a maths nerd. Still am.

Girlchild in a hurry.

Life was never fast enough.
I wanted to gallop, wanted to fly.
Feel the wind run its fingers through my hair.

I'd never been any farther from home than our annual beach
holiday at my cousin's home in Florianópolis.

Happily squinting into sunlight dancing across the crystal lip of green-grey waves.

My one and only plane flight was to Rio de Janeiro, less than two hours away.
Knowing then that such wondrous places existed, my mind was awash with bright and fragrant possibilities.
Travelling the world was all I dreamed about.

I yearned to touch and taste the faraway.

My wholly unoriginal plan was to explore the USA after I graduated from university.
Undertake further studies at an American college. Perhaps.
Peel back the Hollywood veneer, disarm a global superpower, hang with DiCaprio.
Do a little shopping.

Days before I booked my plane ticket to Orlando – to begin my Grand Tour of North America – I caught up with an old high school friend from Caxias.
Marcos, a gay Catholic who always seemed to be a step ahead of the rest of us, had just returned from a year in Australia.
When Marcos gushed about Sydney, he shone from the neck up.
'Beautiful beaches, clean streets, incredible wildlife, amazing nightlife, gorgeous surfers,' he said. 'And no guns.'

'Heaven on earth.'

I tore up my US itinerary.

19.

I'd taken English lessons in Brazil for twelve, no, fifteen years.
Straight As in my Cambridge University English proficiency
exams.
More importantly, I'd watched a lot of *Seinfeld* reruns.
Maybe too many.

But I'd never had a single conversation in English with a native
speaker. Not one.

When I touched down in Sydney and had no choice but to speak
English, I was astonished to discover that I was actually fluent.

At least by Australian standards.

Having lived my whole life in the Atlantic Forest, the South
Pacific was a revelation.
Bright blue sky, green-blue sea, shimmering gold sand.

Sydney is a city of white teeth and suntanned legs.

Australians seemed happy, relaxed, open.
Always ready to have fun.
Easy smiles, no pretence.
'No worries.'

It was all there, waiting for me.
New school. New job. New friends.
New life.

I wanted to embrace every possibility.

A ravenous young woman of the world ordering one of
everything on the menu.
Each bite tasted sweeter than the last.

Then I kissed Byron.

18.

We connected via a dating app.
Nothing special at first. Just having fun.
Flirting, feeling each other out. Looking for red flags.

In his profile photo Byron looked handsome, but not too
handsome.
I liked that.
He had a kind and honest face.
I liked that even more.

Our first date. A Friday night in early spring.
The evening was surprisingly cool. Cold, actually.

So much for a sexy summer dress.
I wore jeans and a black polo neck, beneath a black faux-leather
coat.
The only skin I was prepared to reveal were glimpses of ankles
and toes, courtesy of my strappy heels.

I was excited but kept my expectations grounded in the dismal
reality of online dating: 10% glimmer of potential, 30% so
fucking boring, 60% creeps.

We met in The Rocks, Sydney's historic waterfront.
Cobblestone laneways and weathered colonial buildings.

A charming tourist trap built with blocks of gingerbread coloured sandstone.

Overcrowded? Yes.
A little dingy and dangerous? Maybe.
Romantic? Absolutely.

Byron was waiting for me at the espresso martini bar I'd told him I wanted to try.
When he stood up, he was even taller than I expected.
Like, tall-tall.
I was glad I'd worn high heels.

He was also wearing jeans, with a crisp white linen shirt, a dark sports coat and blue loafers.
We'd both nailed the smart casual look, I guess.

Byron's expensively tailored jacket made him seem older than he was. More money than style.
Perhaps he couldn't shake off the young executive look.
But it all worked.

Visually at least, it made sense that we were together.
We had a couple's vibe.

Good start.

Byron worked in investment banking; his office was quite close by.

I'm sure he looked gorgeous in a business suit.
So, I was impressed when he admitted he'd gone home to shower and change before our date.

He smelled summery and fresh.
A warm beach covered in flowers.

Byron carried himself with gentle confidence, but also seemed a little nervous.
He stumbled at the opening bell by telling me I was so much more attractive in person than in my dating app profile photo.

This cliché is the new normal for online dating greetings, unless the first impression is 'complete trainwreck'.
In which case, you would hear something like 'You look so different from your profile photo, in a good way.'
Meaning, 'In a very bad way.'

I smiled and shrugged off his nothing-compliment.
But then, as we small-talked through our happy awkwardness,
I caught Byron staring at me, his eyes alight.
Like I was the most beautiful woman he had ever seen.
The most beautiful anything that ever lived.
Which, in that moment, standing next to him, was exactly how I felt.

All the silly, funny, saucy banter we'd shared online suddenly evaporated.
Poof. Gone.

The realness of finally being together hit home.

Our date mattered to him.
It mattered to me.

17.

Byron was a modern gentleman.

Polite, courteous, but still a little entitled to being in charge.
He'd assumed command of our date, laying out every step of his
carefully structured program for our evening.

It all sounded lovely, and I appreciated the effort.
But it's not in my Brazilian nature to be controlled.
I changed his masterplan on the spot.
Threw out every single detail.
And he loved it.

We talked and laughed, drank our cocktails, and wanted more.
More everything.

It felt like the beginning of … something.

Instead of walking to the boujee Japanese restaurant Byron had
originally chosen, I put him in a taxi and took him to a vegan
yum cha restaurant in the shadow of St Mary's Cathedral, just
across from Hyde Park.
All the trees were wrapped in sparkling warm-gold fairy lights.

Byron wasn't vegan – at all – but he was hungry and
openminded, and he trusted me to guide him through the
menu.

The food was delicious.
The conversation wonderful.

A Brazilian and a South African who shared a love of Sydney.
We both looked at our adopted country through the fresh eyes of
outsiders whose foreign accents belied a natural affinity for the
Australian way of life.

We were already used to getting sunburnt on Christmas Day.
We both believed that flip-flops were appropriate footwear for all
occasions.
Though I was guilty of calling them slippers and Byron
occasionally called them *plakkies*, which made me snort-laugh.

We both raved about Cadbury chocolate, Tim Tams and, to my
surprise, the coffee; Italians may have invented the cappuccino,
but Aussies perfected it.

Byron was alone in his affection for Vegemite.
Neither of us cared about cricket or rugby.
Byron preferred golf.
And I grew up watching my local soccer team.
'Come on Grêmio – Tricolor for life!'

I felt safe and happy in Australia.
I felt safe and happy with Byron.

There was no compulsion to impress each other.
No need to obscure or embellish.

We just talked, openly and honestly, at turns serious, silly and surprising.

I was comfortable, it was intoxicating, it was fun.

Every flavour of laughter.

We both asked a great many questions.

Curious, probing, but always respectful.

The deeper we went, the better it got.

Byron enjoyed my crazy stories from Brazil.

He had gleeful empathy for the entry level jobs I'd taken to get through university.

My shared-living misadventures in Sydney were also painfully familiar terrain.

I loved hearing about Byron's childhood in South Africa.

His family emigrated to Australia when he was a teenager.

It hadn't been an easy transition.

His parents' struggle in their adopted country had motivated him to complete a degree in finance in Sydney and a master's degree in London.

It was obvious that he worked incredibly hard to make the most of the opportunities he'd been given.

We had a lot in common, especially in our appreciation for the sacrifices our parents had made for us.

I saw him brighten whenever I spoke about my amazing mother.

Byron was very close to his parents.

Family was important to him.

I was falling for him.
There was nothing I could do about it.

We didn't get up to leave until a tired waiter shyly told us they were closing.
It was almost midnight.

I remember walking underneath the giant illuminated fig tree in the restaurant's courtyard, hoping that Byron would hold my hand.
He didn't.

But when we reached the top of the stairs and stood before the gothic doorway of St Mary's Cathedral, aglow in the floodlights, we caught each other staring.

Wanting, waiting.

He asked my permission without saying a word.
Brought me close, held me in his arms, and kissed me.
And I kissed him back.
Softly.
Then less softly.

I didn't feel the cold anymore.

16.

The rush of heat in my mouth.
Deafening trill of my heartbeat.
A bumblebee dancing on a snare drum.

But then what?

We stayed pressed against each other.
Uncertain, excited by what our immediate future might hold.

I looked up and I saw the cathedral's twin sandstone spires
reaching into the heavens.
As if these giant golden arms were summoning every star in the
night sky to bear witness to new love.

☆ ☆

For want of courage and a better idea, we disentangled and
agreed to a nightcap at The Lobo.
A quirky underground Cuban bar, a few blocks beyond Hyde
Park.

The dark stairwell descending into The Lobo smelled warm and
spicy.
The bar itself was a baroque jungle.
Glinting bottles surrounded by colourful curios, gaudy
tchotchkes and nowhere-souvenirs.
Every object backlit by small, flickering candles, which made the
room sway and dance.

It was hard to hear anything above the hum and hustle of a
Friday night crowd unbuttoning their power suits.

After the quiet sanctity of our first kiss, it was all a bit too much.

But we slid-squeezed into a corner booth and ordered rum
cocktails.
Mine was made with pine syrup and fresh lime juice and garnished
with a cute little toy dinosaur that I popped into my handbag.
Delicious and adorable.

At first, we just shy-smiled. Staring at each other.
As if speaking might wipe the kiss from our lips.

In any case, talking was difficult until our social volume
normalised.
Slowly we were won over by the bar's heady ambience.
Sugary rum coursing through our bloodstreams.

Our energy changed.

The inescapably noisy crowd seemed both omnipresent and
strangely distant.
A blurred background.

It was just Byron and me.

Wilfully lost in an imagined public celebration of secret intimacy.
Which makes no sense, I know.
But it was late, and dreamy, and the night was ours.

Conversation was livelier now. We laughed louder.

Travel?
God yes, we both loved travel, exploring, nature.
Let's go.

And food? We loved food.
I had given up meat just a few months before but, instead of
feeling deprived, I'd discovered a realm of hidden flavours.
Byron was happily dubious, but genuinely intrigued.

Music?
We were both into the Australian and French electronic dance
scene.
Byron was a big fan of Lane 8 and Daft Punk, and I had an
aural crush on Bag Raiders, Pnau and Phoenix.
EDM simpatico.

We didn't agree on everything, but our differences resulted in
faux arguments that made us laugh even harder.
I can't recall another date that was this much fun.
Not even close.

There wasn't much room to move in our little booth.
Overexcited legs knotting into macramé beneath the table.
We were together now, and the possibilities of 'us' were growing
exponentially.

I could feel my pupils widening, all the light pouring in.
The most wonderful feeling, most wonderful time.
Magical, even.
But also excruciating.

I wanted that second kiss.

◇

Suddenly it was 2 am.

The bar staff called time and politely emptied us out onto the chilled pavement.

A new moon balanced atop the city skyline.

Standing still on the footpath, holding each other as a river of people rushed past, we kissed in a puddle of neon light.

15.

I didn't want the night to end but also, perhaps for the first time in my life, I didn't want to move too fast.

There was something special in our connection that needed nurturing.
Worth waiting for.

Byron proposed that we go to his apartment in Double Bay and continue our evening over a glass of wine.
I wanted to say yes so badly. I knew I couldn't trust myself.

Thankfully, I had a rejection-free excuse.

I was supposed to be cat-sitting a sweet black and ginger tabby, named Lea, for a friend of mine who was out of town for a few days.
I was staying at his apartment in Chippendale to ensure Lea was well looked after.

I've always had a thing for cats.

Time and space had dissolved into blissful meaninglessness during our date.
I was jarred into reality with the realisation that I'd been away from Lea far longer than I'd expected.

I needed to get back, make sure she had enough food and water and wasn't stuck atop a bookshelf or trapped inside a kitchen drawer.

Intrepid little whiskered fool that she was.

Byron accepted my regrets with grace and charm.
Without missing a beat, he offered to escort me home.
I was quietly pleased by the tiny pang of disappointment he couldn't quite conceal.

There was little chance of a vacant taxi at that hour.
And the idea of stalling our romantic momentum to wait for an Uber in the cold was just … No.
We wanted this night to end on our terms.
Fireworks all the way.

Sensing our shared need to maintain the emotional trajectory,
Byron suggested we walk.
Or maybe it was my idea.
A brisk twenty minutes to Chippendale from the bar.
A touch longer in high heels.

Byron wrapped my hand in his.
If my feet hurt, I didn't notice.

Lea was waiting up like an anxious aunt, or a distraught chaperone who'd fallen asleep on the job.

The temptation to invite Byron inside was strong, stronger than gravity.
Thankfully he had no expectations, and if he did, he didn't press his case.
We said our goodbyes on the doorstep, as Lea laced figure eights around my ankles.

I kissed Byron goodnight and then, as he turned to leave, called him back to place my cocktail dinosaur in his hand.
A silly gesture.
But I wanted Byron to wake up with physical evidence of our date.

To remind him that we had happened.
To know that the feelings we'd shared were real.

He laughed, I smiled.
And he was gone.

I saw my breath as I sighed.

I soothed and fed Lea, kicked off my shoes and called my mum.
She was taking her lunch break in Caxias do Sul.

I let her know I'd been out on a date with someone very special.

'He isn't classically handsome,' I told her.
'But he's the most beautiful man I've ever met.'

14.

THREE DATES

Awake earlier than planned.
Lea made sure of it.

My nervous half-asleep thumbs were still composing a hopefully
funny and not too flirtatious pseudo-casual thank-you message to
Byron when he texted me.

My blood jumped. Lea jumped.
A visceral cloudburst of caffeinated fizz.
I needed to go to the bathroom. But I didn't, couldn't budge.

There was a flurry of digital back-and-forth.
Every new message sparkled, a tiny present to unwrap with a
happy squeal.

Byron invited me to lunch the next day.

We were daylight official.
Happy for the whole world to look on with envy and amusement.

We met at the Empire Lounge, at the Sydney seaplane terminal
in Rose Bay.
Cloud-free skies, infinite blue.
From our table we could see past Shark Island, all the way across
Sydney Harbour.

Byron watched me closely as I read the one-page menu in detail.
Checking and rechecking the cryptic crossword of ingredients,
weighing up my choices.
I'm not sure what kind of interpretive dance my eyebrows were
doing but, when I finally looked up, Byron was trying not to laugh.

When he realised I was searching for elusive vegan options, he
tried to help.
Then he went inside to speak to the manager to ensure I got
exactly what I wanted.

It was too much, a silly heroic gesture, adorable overkill.
I never want to be the kind of person who makes a fuss, causes a
scene about what I eat.
But, you know, sweet.
Byron cared about me.

My happiness was his priority.

Our Sunday was low-key lovely.
So very different from our splashy night on the town, but equally
enjoyable.
I found Byron easy to talk to.
Easy to spend time with.

Seaplanes wallowed in and out of the terminal.
We ate, drank wine, talked and talked.

The sky turned marigold.
Then blood orange.
Then indigo.

The minute I got home I began planning our next romantic adventure.

When you meet someone, and the attraction is mutual, but everything that needs to be known remains unknown, it's hard to discern real chemistry from fantasy.
Genuine romantic potential from undiluted desire.
Everything is seen through the filter of a daydream.

What I do know is that a week is a long time to wait.

Torture is far too strong a word, but I can't immediately think of a better one.

We wanted to see each other but we couldn't.
Byron was busy at work and travelled constantly.
I had a demanding supply chain job that required total concentration.
A single error, hiding amid a thousand tiny details tumbling across my computer screen, could cost the company millions.

Byron's name was constantly on my lips.

I thought about him during workouts, meetings and meals.
Awake, asleep.
Everywhere, always.

We texted each other constantly, for no reason.
I loved it.

Weekdays became vast and shapeless things.
Counting down the hours till we'd be together again.

Our smiles reunited on Sydney Harbour the following Friday
after work.

Boarding the Manly ferry at dusk.
All eyes on us.
Two lovers amid a sluggish cargo of tired commuters.

An endless leather ribbon of fruit bats streaming high overhead,
beyond the fading growl of the metropolis.

We swayed together, in time with the pitch and roll of the swell.
My head on Byron's shoulder, savouring the warm notes of my
lover's cologne and the cool salt air.

A jewel of a city as our backdrop.
Proud and electric.
The Sydney Harbour Bridge floodlights and countless twinkling
apartment windows painted the living sea with constellations of
shimmer and brilliance.

Drowsy silver gulls, startled off the water by the ferry's bow
wave, flew past us.
Wings and bellies white-hot-bright as their feathers mirrored the
wild glare of the stern light.
Then instantly and absolutely vanishing into the darkness, like a
magic trick.

The perfect way to unwind after five days of corporate grind.
Sure.
But it felt like something bigger.
A cinematic denouement from Hollywood's Golden Age.
A romantic escape, rehearsal elopement … call it what you will.

We disembarked, wide-eyed and full-hearted.
Happy tourists in our illuminated backyard.

Nothing fancy.
Drinks at Manly Wharf.
Veggie burgers from The Hold.

We walked down The Corso, from harbour to sea, hand in hand.
Light and breezy back and forth.
Pretending not to stare at each other.
Totally staring at each other.

We kissed beneath the Norfolk Island pines by the beach, to the
applause of breaking waves.

It was simple, and pure, and lovely.

Back in the sleepless city, the agony of parting.
As we said and kissed our goodbyes, Byron placed a small velvet
bag in my hand.
Inside was an exquisite little porcelain dinosaur.

His reply to the plastic trinket I'd given him as a binding token of our first date.

Byron knew exactly what I'd meant, and he wanted me to know he felt the same.
He'd fallen for me too.

All the feelings.

I called my mum.

Love compels you to do the strangest things.

On our fourth date, I told Byron I wanted to cook him dinner at his apartment which, unlike mine, was flatmate free.
Yes, everything would be vegan.
I promised it would also be delicious.
A bold statement for someone who didn't cook that often, or that well.

This would be my first visit to Byron's home, so I spent longer getting ready than I should have.

I went with a little black and white dress.
Summery and chic, very French.
Totally impractical in the kitchen.
Worth it.

It was already 7.30 pm by the time I had dragged the heavy bags straining with dinner ingredients to Byron's apartment in Double Bay.

I'd also brought all the necessary cookware and utensils, as I suspected that Byron, who usually ate on the run, to and from his office, wasn't entirely sure where his kitchen was located, or what it was for.

As host and executive chef, I took charge of our evening.
Byron, a guest in his own home, opened a bottle of sauvignon blanc.
It seemed rude not to have a glass.
Then a second.

Our private happy hour sailed by before we realised that most Sydney households were already washing up and we hadn't even started cooking.

The vegan menu I'd set for us was just two courses.
Lasagne, followed by ice-cream and cookies.
Too easy. Right?

Well, it took forever.

Lasagne has been made successfully since the 13th century.
Pasta, tomatoes, cheese and béchamel sauce which is, so I'm told, the most basic of all sauces.
To be fair, vegan cheese and vegan béchamel sauce are a tad temperamental.

My date became my sous chef and the two of us were fussing
and crashing around in the kitchen for an age.

Nothing was mixing properly.
We ended up using the blender so often and for so long that
Byron's downstairs neighbour stormed up the stairs to bang on
the door and shout at us for making too much noise.
Our persistent giggling probably didn't ease tensions.

When I'd completed the multiple layers of pasta, sauce and
cheese I realised we had made far too much sauce.
There was enough béchamel left over to baptise a child.

It was 10.30 pm before I put the lasagne into the oven.
At 11.15 pm our main course still didn't seem done.
So, we waited.
And waited.

We finally sat down for dinner at 11.45 pm.

It didn't look good.
My lasagne appeared both scorched and somehow resistant to
heat – a wilted throw cushion that had hidden in a casserole dish
to escape a house fire.
'I'll bet it tastes great though,' said Byron encouragingly.

It did not.

The béchamel sauce was no longer the villain.
Despite doubling the recommended cooking time, the lasagne
pasta sheets were still as resolute as linoleum tiles.

We gingerly nibble-slurped the hot sauce and cheese around great rectangles of bulletproof pasta.

Byron opened another, now painfully necessary bottle of white wine.
He was attempting to compose a compliment to the chef when neither of us could hold in our laughter any longer.

We laughed until tears ran down our cheeks and the downstairs neighbour banged on their ceiling in protest.

It was the perfect way to end a very funny evening.
Or at least it would have been if I wasn't so stubborn.

I doubled down on dinner salvage.
'Once more unto the breach'. We had to make dessert.
Marching back into the kitchen to mix and fold cookie dough.
The oven was turned back on.

This time everything went smoothly and, just before or after 2 am, we sat down to devour deliciously warm, homemade cookies.

I didn't go home that night.

13.

I'd essentially fallen out of the sky.
When I'd stepped off the plane in Sydney my social circle was a
doughnut.
I knew no one.

Every friendship was freshly forged, shiny and new.
And making new friends is hard.
For anyone, anywhere.
But when you move to a new school, new job, new city, new
country ... where do you even begin?

Assuming you speak the language, there remains an invisible
minefield of subtle social cues, opaque interpersonal politics,
local tastes and taboos, secret cliques, unwritten rules.

To be fair, there are far fewer social barriers in Australia.

It's not nearly as diverse or as inclusive as Brazil or, I suspect, as
easy-going Australians would like to imagine.
Foreigners and new arrivals are still regarded with a degree of
suspicion.
As are vegans, teetotallers and intellectuals.
But it's considered gauche, if not downright un-Australian, to
care too deeply about religion or politics, which opens a lot of
doors that you'll find closed elsewhere.

You'll frequently hear that money doesn't matter either.
But that's obviously not true.
Here, or anywhere.

What I loved most about Australia is that so long as you can
laugh at yourself and you turn up with a bottle of wine in hand,
or a case of beer, you're generally made to feel welcome.
Australian egalitarianism is found in a frosted glass.

But turning up can prove difficult.
Especially if, like me, you don't have a lot of money and don't
drive.

I owned a nice little car, once.

When I first arrived in Sydney I bought a second-hand white
Mercedes hatchback that looked like a shiny snowball.
And, for a brief window of time, I possessed a learner driver's
licence.

But I was pulled over by the police for talking on my mobile
phone while driving, not having a fully licensed driver in the car
with me, and not using my indicator.
There was also a fourth traffic violation that I can't recall …
Let's assume it was for 'being too damn sexy behind the wheel'.

For my sins I received $1200 in fines and an invitation to catch
the bus indefinitely.

Little surprise then that my closest friends were also those closest to me.

Literally.

Friends from uni, friends from work and my flatmates.

Suffice it to say, falling in love with Byron opened a whole new world for me.

12.

Byron invited me to see The Chainsmokers, who were performing at the Sydney Showground.

I was over the moon until he said we would start the evening with pre-show drinks in Double Bay, where we would be joined by twelve of his best friends.

This was my society debut.
Ready or not.

Laura, my New Zealander buddy from work, who was always up for anything, agreed to come along for moral support.
But she was working late and would have to meet us at the show.

So, it was settled.
I would face the bankers' inquisition on my own.

There's a point where excitement and fear become indistinguishable.
And that point was located just behind my sternum.

Me, a timid little bunny? Hardly.

I loved meeting new people because I love people. Always have.
I'm never the life of the party but I genuinely enjoy being social.
I'll talk to anyone, anywhere, anytime.

Everyone has something interesting to share if you give them a chance to speak.

But what Byron and I had together was as fresh and new and perfect as a naked baby.
So precious.

I was a little nervous.
More than a little, maybe.

I just didn't want anything to go wrong.

Byron's friends were beautiful.
As in 'Wow!' beautiful.

The best and brightest from every continent.

The men were tall and handsome.
The women, statuesque and gorgeous.
And smart. So smart.

They all worked in finance, like Byron.
And they were clearly very good at what they did.
Even dressed casually for a dance party it was obvious they had real money.
Fancy shoes, chunky watches, earrings that caught every beam of light.
None of my friends in Porto Alegre could dream of such wealth, let alone wear it out in public.

As the door closed behind me, everyone turned and looked down
to see who I was.
I instantly felt out of place.
Too short, too bohemian, too poor.

But I knew I was a force to be reckoned with.
I spoke music and maths as well as anybody.
Plus, my boyfriend was the host.

Boyfriend.
What a big little word that is.

Byron spotted me across the room.
In three strides he was beside me and gathered me up to kiss hello.
I immediately felt taller.

We moved around the party as Byron made introductions.
It was the United Nations of attractive young bankers.
Most were lovely.
Some less so.

Hugh, a sharply dressed American, seemed wholly disinterested
in my life and death so far.
He suffered from resting disapproval face.
Childhood must have been a hoot.

Margo, an Aussie redhead with a tan who looked like an athlete,
seemed a little cold at first. She sized me up like an opponent
she'd already beaten.

And Olivia, a willowy blonde who'd artfully shackled three
white gold Cartier Love bracelets so that they didn't quite

obscure a minimalist wrist tattoo of the word 'étoile'. Olivia might have been mistaken for a fashion model except she could prove Gödel's Incompleteness Theorem and yet, somehow, she seemed even more nervous than I was.

Byron's closest friend, JP, looked a little wounded when we were introduced.
His smile seemed strained, and he quickly turned away.
Byron excused himself and went after him. So did Olivia.
I was left wondering what had just happened when Grace swooped in to rescue me.

11.

'Don't worry, he'll get over it,' Grace assured me in perfect Portuguese.

'JP is the absolute best. He's just sulking because you stole his wingman.'

Brazilian by birth, British by nature, Grace had been raised all around the world, including previous stints in Australia and New Zealand, and had spent most of her life in England.

Tall, dark and gorgeous, she spoke four languages fluently and could order cocktails in several more.

Her green eyes dimmed the lights in every room she walked into.

Grace explained how she and Byron met as classmates at the London School of Economics, while they were completing their master's degrees.

Grace was married at the time, she told me, but had fallen in love with a younger man, Byron's college roommate, Colin.

So, she'd shrugged off her marriage and followed her heart.

Grace pointed out Colin, standing at the bar.
I could see the appeal.

Grace brought me up to speed on Byron's inner circle in less time than it took to drain a glass of champagne.

Margo hadn't had a boyfriend in years.
Taking Byron off the market wasn't the best way to add my name to her Christmas card list.

Olivia was a beautiful mess.
She'd had a fling with JP, a one-night stand, nothing serious, at least to JP, who was rebounding from a divorce.

Hugh was both a semi-genius and a semi-jerk who didn't get out much.
About as charismatic as a face drawn on a thumb.
But he was a good friend when it really mattered, according to Byron.

Grace had me in stitches with her inside gossip about the group and their shared adventures.
She cut her friends open like a juicy mango, exposing all their sticky secrets.

Their sleek, intimidating veneer of sophistication was apparently an illusion, just as their idea of adulting was pure make-believe.
Peter Pan in Louboutins.

They were young workaholics.
Always full throttle. No idea how to use the brakes.
Big kids with big brains and big toys.

Nerds who'd won at life.
I kind of loved that about them.

Their lifestyle was as exciting as it was unsustainable, and I suspect they all knew it.
Burnout was inevitable.
A mercy, probably.
But until then they were going all in.

Byron and his friends were 21st-century fiscal samurai with a gift for bloodless analysis and an extreme tolerance for risk.

I was in awe of this, even seduced by it.

But also, at some level, a little uneasy.

In the face of Grace's unflinching honesty I was scrambling to re-evaluate Byron's true nature.

I knew his profession. I knew he had money.

But this setting. This crowd.

Beautiful and exciting.

Yet emotionally inconsistent with the Byron I'd come to know.

How much did I really know about him?

Was he truly the man I'd fallen for?

Byron's friends were amazing, I liked them, I did.

Most of them anyway.

However, their posturing forced me to see my new boyfriend in a new light.

Also, wake-up call – what about my own character, my own values?

What did I truly care about?

What was I looking for in this relationship?

As I looked around the room, the bold red question I couldn't shake was this:

Did the all-consuming drive for high performance, in a purely transactional realm, leave any room to truly connect with someone, to care enough, to sacrifice enough, to love enough, to build something real together?

With a grin, Grace acknowledged that white picket fences were not prized in her world.
But she assured me that Byron's life goals transcended the arena of commerce.
His domestic dreams mattered far more to him than money.
Money was just a tool.

If I could believe her, and god knows I wanted to, Byron was a big-hearted banking anomaly.

Yes, he could pull the trigger on a killer deal without blinking, but he was also a sensitive soul who radiated kindness, empathy and decency.
Which is why everyone liked Byron, and why Grace admired and adored him.

In a cruel world of Lestats, he was a Louis.

Grace and I gleefully employed bilingual obfuscation.
Upbeat party banter in plain English.
Secret jokes, at the expense of other guests, in Portuguese.

We were engaged in a conspiratorial giggle-fest when Byron and Colin vectored towards us with brightly coloured drinks.

As we broke our clinch to rejoin the party, Grace leaned in.
'Don't worry,' she whispered, for the second time. 'Everyone is going to love you. You are exactly what Byron needed. You're good for him.'

A sweet but strange compliment.
I only kind of liked it.

Within half an hour I realised I was wrong.

I wasn't the only one anxious about being evaluated that night.
After Grace put me at ease, I was better able to read the room.
Byron's friends seemed genuinely worried about what I thought
of them.
Too funny.

If you've ever sucked in your belly for a photo, then you know
how good it feels to finally let it all hang out.
Well, that was me.

Their intimidating swagger and volume was just posturing and
puffery.
The pseudo-confidence of answering a question with a question.
They wore Rolexes on their wrists, not Wonder Woman's
Bracelets of Submission.
If you stood your ground and engaged with them, they blinked.

I saw through these jet-setting nerd-babies and I wasn't afraid.
Quite the opposite.
I liked them for who they were, not who they pretended to be.
I belonged in the room.

More importantly, I was in love.

I was in love and I was ready to have the night of my life.

10.

Colin checked his phone and smiled.
He opened the door to peek outside, then stepped out of the apartment.
A minute later he ducked back in and called out, 'Are we doing this?'
As one, we all screamed 'YES!'

With Byron holding one hand and Grace holding the other, I stumble-skip-skidded out the door and down the stairs.

The driveway was an obsidian river of limousines.
Byron and I piled in with Grace, Colin, JP, Olivia and Hugh.

The pre-show party continued on wheels.
More champagne.
More stories.
Music turned up. We all knew the words.

Quite a bit nicer than taking the bus.

As our destination drew near, JP and Olivia started handing out party drugs.
Tiny pink pills. The ones that Aussies call 'disco biscuits'.
Byron and I shrugged at each other and took one each.
I saw Hugh take two. So at least he knew his face had a problem.

We'd barely walked through the main entrance of the concert
venue when Laura hug-tackled me.
A joyful wrecking ball of love – she made Byron and Grace jump.
Olivia offered Laura a pink pill, but she was already buzzing
and didn't need it.

I was so happy to see her.

We all stood together, facing the stage.
Excited, so excited.
As if waiting to witness the first sunrise of our entire lives.

The house lights dimmed, and the crowd erupted.

Piercing hum of a synthesiser.
A single note.
Volume building.
Syncopated rattle of electronic percussion.

One spotlight beam cutting through the fog machine haze.
Then another, and another, and another, and another, and,
and, and … suddenly Alex and Drew, The Chainsmokers DJ
demigods, appeared in a cloudburst of starlight.

The bassline dropped and 10,000 souls jumped into another
dimension.

The show was spectacular.
Gigantic video projections, the incandescent roar of
pyrotechnics, dazzling pulses of coloured light.

And the music, oh my heavens, the music.
Gritty cosmic poetry as atomic melodies.
Loud enough to realign the chakras of the gods.
Time itself started to dance.

It was sublime.

We danced until we were drenched in sweat, and then we kept
dancing.
The crowd throbbing in unison.
One gigantic heart.

Byron and I were dancing and laughing and shouting the
lyrics.
I danced with Laura, Grace and Colin, then JP and Olivia,
Grace and Byron, a scrum of overexcited strangers, then Laura
again.

This is why I loved EDM – the beautiful madness of
omnidirectional technicolour joy.
Even Hugh's face was having the best time ever.

Laura and I took turns sitting on Byron's shoulders so we could
see the stage above the psychedelic mosh.
Poor Byron, our sweaty thighs wrapped around his neck.
He loved it.

I pulled out my phone. Wanted to video what I was seeing,
hearing and feeling.
It was hopeless.

Like trying to capture the power of Iguaçu Falls with a
teaspoon.
You just had to be there.

And I was.

When The Chainsmokers played their hit 'Roses', my heart
caught fire.
I shouted at Byron, 'This is us! This is our song!'

> *Oh, I'll be your daydream,*
> *I'll be your favorite things*
> *We could be beautiful*
> *Get drunk on the good life,*
> *I'll take you to paradise*
> *Say you'll never let me go.*

The song stayed in my head as we drove home.
Exhausted, elated.
I could hear it playing when we made love.
I could feel it, like fireworks under my skin.

> *Say you'll never let me go.*
> *Say you'll never let me go.*

I called my mum the next day to tell her all about the amazing
show, the new friends I'd made, and how we'd danced all night.

Mum was confused.

'But you hate dancing. You haven't danced since you were a young girl,' she said.

This caught me off-guard.

But I knew she was right.

'You used to love dancing,' she continued.

'You were even in a dance group for a year or two with your closest girlfriends, when you were little. Do you remember?'

'And then, one day … One day, you just stopped.'

'And there was nothing I could do, nothing anyone could do or say to get you to dance again.'

'If you're dancing now, then I have to believe it's because you're in love.'

She paused.

'True love.'

9.

Falling in love with Byron was an accidental dream.
But I still had other dreams.

From the day I first breathed Australian air, I wanted to live in
Bondi.
Home to the most popular beach in the country.
Perhaps the most famous beach in the world … after
Copacabana.

⟨⟨⟨⟨⟩⟩⟩⟩

BONDI

Few words can ruin my appetite for fun like 'city beach'.

In most parts of the world, including Brazil, I envision broken
pipes belching raw sewage into the sea. Dead fish and drowned
rats rolling in the shore break.
Greasy shorebirds and sharks eating the freshest garbage.
Cockroaches devouring the rest.

Bondi Beach is an exception.
Imagine a miniature Ipanema licked clean by angels.

A perfect crescent of golden sand, right on the edge of Australia's
largest city.
Bright blue ocean tinted with a dawn splash of emerald.

It's hard to describe a place with such universal appeal that is so uniquely Australian.
Old money and new money, but not Malibu.
Traditions and trendsetters, but not Montauk.
One festival after another, but not Ibiza.
Beautiful people and beautiful views, but it's not South Beach.

This sun-kissed corner of Sydney's Eastern Suburbs is more than just sand and surf.
Bondi has a heartbeat, a creative soul.
It's truly alive thanks to energetic residents and young entrepreneurs.
Quirky boutiques, public art, bars and restaurants and music venues, a charming and dynamic café culture.

And Gertrude & Alice, quite possibly the nicest bookshop in the world.

There's a real sense of community in Bondi.
Locals come in every flavour, but they all look out for each other.
It isn't a hygienically sealed utopia.
But, in their own way, everyone inside the Bondi Bubble champions a healthy lifestyle and a healthy environment.

I don't mean blanched kale smoothies in recyclable cups, though that is a thing.
I mean a foundational commitment to the vitality of people and place.
The local council installed a solar-powered stormwater filtration and storage system underground to save precious rainwater and make dolphins happier.

I loved it.

Of course, paradise isn't free.
The average annual rent in Bondi is a house deposit in most
other cities.
And the average house deposit in Bondi is a healthy kidney in a
bucket of ice sold on the black market in Singapore.

Which explained why so many of Byron's friends lived there.

Realty hypervigilance.
I was constantly checking the new share accommodation listings.
A cat with her face pressed against a fishbowl.

I eventually found an almost perfect apartment.
Good size, reasonably priced.
Great location.
Just a ten-minute walk downhill to the beach.

My potential flatmate seemed like a decent guy.

Interview went well. Papers were signed. Hands were shaken.
Laura helped me move.

Summer was an aquamarine blur.

My new flatmate, Joey, was roughly my age.
A bit of a house mouse, but nice.

He and I would sometimes walk to the beach together.
His only crime was wearing designer jean shorts.

Byron and I worked late on weekdays, always.
Between Monday and Friday our relationship was sustained by
text messages.
Très millennial.

The upside was that I had time to seek out neighbourhood
hotspots and catch up with all my new friends.
Drinks and nibbles with Grace.
Clubbing with Laura.
The occasional dinner with Olivia, who was very sweet once you
got to know her.

Ah, but the weekends.
The weekends were for lovers.
Ours alone.

Dinners, concerts, movies, parties.
Big nights out.
Quiet nights in.

Wildly romantic escapades. Lazy snuggle-fests.
Making oversized plans, freestyling without a clue.
Always exploring, making memories.
Loving love.

Friday through Sunday, we generally stayed at Byron's place in
Double Bay.
But every now and then, Byron would submit to his oversized
feet hanging over the end of my normal-sized bed.

In the morning, Joey's sad-startled eyes would lift from behind the television and track us from my bedroom to the front door. Funny-awkward.

◇

The festive season was almost upon us, but no one was prepared to wait for it.
Australians celebrate the approach of a major celebration like no one else.
The lead-up to a national holiday triggers wholesale rejection of the Protestant work ethic as a national priority.

Pre-holiday party after pre-holiday party.
Then holiday party after holiday party.
Each bigger and sillier and crazier than the last.
A little like *Carnaval* in Brazil, but slightly less public nudity and almost no one has rhythm.

So. Much. Fun.

I was getting more and more comfortable in Byron's larger-than-life world.
I didn't feel overwhelmed or out of place at all anymore.
His brash friends either liked me or feared me.
I was fine either way.
There was nothing that could rattle me now.

Until there was.

8.

Byron pulled the rug out from under my size nines with two
thrilling questions.

Would I join him for Christmas dinner with his parents?
His parents!
And … Would I go to South Africa with him?

The implications of each invitation were not yet entirely clear,
but I know I squealed the word 'Yes' like a mouse who'd won the
national cheese lottery.

Absolutely Yes, and Yes!

I would have gladly agreed to camp on one of Jupiter's lesser
moons, Byron had only to ask.
But I was not the only person Byron had to ask.

He'd been planning the trip to South Africa with Grace, Colin,
JP and Margo for a very long time.
Well before he and I had started dating.
Byron felt he needed to get their blessing for me to join them.

This stung a little.

On the one hand, he loved me enough to want me to meet his
mum and dad.
Spend Christmas Day with his family.

Yet, he still felt he needed his friends' permission for me to go on holiday with them.

I was confused, but I tried to see the situation from his point of view.
When Byron had originally made these plans with his friends, he, Margo and JP were all single.
Adding a second couple to the mix changed the dynamic.
It would be a very different vacation now.

Seeking 'permission' from JP and Margo jarred my heart, as neither of them had warmed to me.
I guess I should have been grateful he didn't have to ask Hugh.
That said, I understood that a courtesy call was in order, and I knew Grace and Colin would be there to support me.

I was determined not to let this bring me down.

Being introduced to Mattys and Embeth, Byron's parents, was like meeting celebrities I'd been watching on television for years.
I'd heard so much about them I already knew them.

They hugged me like a long-lost daughter.

Mattys and Embeth lived in Wisemans Ferry, an historic town on the outskirts of Sydney with a population less than my apartment building.
Their beautiful home was immersed in nature and overlooked the great Hawkesbury River.
The air was clean and cool, and smelled like eucalyptus leaves.

Christmas dinner was so fun that we did it twice in twenty-four hours.
Silly hats and all.

Embeth, petite and affectionate, surprised me with a vegan feast on Christmas Eve.
I was so happy I almost cried.
Then, on Christmas Day, we ate a beautiful holiday luncheon outside, on their verandah, overlooking the river.

Mattys, a grizzly bear-sized wine buff, had assembled an enormous cellar of fine wines.
Every bottle had its own backstory.
The frequent suck-pop of corks being pulled became the rhythm section for our Christmas soundtrack.
A raucous choir of colourful wild parrots provided the vocals.

In Brazil we look forward to fireworks at Christmastime, but sipping wine by the river is a family tradition I could happily make my own.

We boarded our flight early the next morning.
Byron wore his goofy reindeer hat; I kept my silly Santa hat on.
It was still Christmas Day in South Africa, and we were determined to keep the holiday spirit alive.

Cape Town took my breath away.
A stunning coastal city wrapped around and between towering mountains.

Almost the exact same latitude as my hometown in Brazil, and my adopted hometown in Australia.

It felt like everything was somehow connected.

I was meant to be here with Byron.

I still didn't know what to expect from JP and Margo.

Byron and I had shared a ride to the airport with Grace and Colin, and I'd barely talked to Margo and JP before we boarded the plane.

But was this because they felt I was intruding on their private holiday, or because we were all nursing festive hangovers?

I couldn't say.

I shouldn't have worried.

JP was simply lovely to me after we touched down.

All of Byron's friends were.

So much so that I wondered if Grace had said something to them.

Margo was more pleasant than usual, while still managing to be an emotional bruiser.

She felt compelled to trump everyone's stories and achievements with her own, which I found belittling and annoying.

The group's collective eyerolling, however, made it clear that I was not alone.

Just Margo being Margo.

I soon gathered that having Margo top your anecdote was, in her own way, a sign of respect, maybe even affection.

So, I guess she'd finally accepted me.

Yay?

Cape Town is a traveller's wonderland.
Everything you could possibly want, and we sampled all of it.
From sea to summit, we frolicked in the sunshine and beneath
the stars.

Meeting Byron's aunts, uncles and cousins, and getting to know
so many of his childhood friends was an especial joy.
His grandparents were so incredibly warm and sweet to me.
I felt I had known and adored them all my life.

After savouring the delights of the coast, Byron led us inland for
a weeklong safari at Manyeleti Game Reserve.
During the day we would set out with local guides to see unique
wildlife in a private nature reserve that was roughly one hundred
times the size of Bondi.
When night fell, we'd retreat to our own little lodge.
Cosy and romantic.

As someone who loves seeing animals wild and free, I was
already beside myself when we saw our first monkeys.
They were so different from the monkeys we have in Brazil.
Bigger and bolder, but just as cheeky and full of mischief.

When we encountered prides of lions, leopards, Cape buffalo,
black rhinos, white rhinos, and my absolute favourite,
elephants … I nearly swooned.

Byron was delighted to see how happy I was, exploring his home
country.

South Africa was a defining moment for Byron and me. Connecting with his family's roots, experiencing the cities and the wild places that gave him his lifelong sense of wonder, pride and purpose, unlocked a hidden part of him that I could now hold in my arms.

If I'd harboured any secret doubts about us being together, they completely vanished in South Africa.

7.

Life was different when we returned to Sydney.

Good different.
Amazing different.

Byron's best friends had become my best friends.
Yes, even Margo.
Don't believe me?
I personally set up a private WhatsApp group for us all called 'Besties', and she used it daily. We all did.

Colin gave me a new nickname, 'Broc'.
And it stuck.

Broc was a playful contraction of broccolini, my favourite vegetable and my go-to order if we dined at a nice restaurant where the menu had no vegan options.
Can't say I was thrilled about the group calling me Broc, but they weren't wrong.
I really do love broccolini.

Grace, Olivia and Margo would text me every day about everything and nothing.
Where should we meet up tonight?
What do you think of this outfit?
I'm getting bangs, am I insane?
You know. Girl stuff.

♪

We all went to see Rüfüs Du Sol perform at Carriageworks.
Once again, we did it in style.
This concert was just as fun as my first show with Byron's
friends, if not more so.
This time, everyone liked me before they started popping party
drugs.

Rüfüs Du Sol and The Chainsmokers had become my two
favourite bands.
Which is saying something because, when I was younger, I
loved the Dave Matthews Band with such undiluted teenage
passion that I secretly got 'Dave Matthews Band' tattooed on
my ankle.
Well, just the initials. DMB.
Which I later realised looked like the abbreviation for 'Dumb'.
The dilemma I faced was that if I tried to remove the tattoo, or
cover it with another tattoo, I'd be publicly admitting that I'd
made a dumb mistake.

I decided to own it.

After South Africa, the only place where my life wasn't looking
up was at home.
Joey, normally such an easygoing flatmate, now seemed jealous
of Byron.

Whenever Byron came around Joey would mumble and sulk-
shuffle around the apartment like a dyspeptic penguin.

I won't flatter myself by suggesting Joey had a crush on me,
maybe he just got sick of me talking about my boyfriend.
Maybe he was tired of sharing his apartment with a third person.
Either way, his behaviour made me feel a little uncomfortable.

I let Byron know I was looking for another apartment in Bondi.
And he let me know there was currently a very attractive
vacancy in Double Bay.
His way of suggesting we move in together.

A very big step to take after only six months.

I called my mum and asked her what I should do.
She simply said, 'I love you.'

'I love you too,' I said, confused. 'But should I move in with
Byron so soon?'

My mum said she didn't know. 'It's not for me to say, Lini. My
own love life is a tapestry of mistakes and wonders.'

My mum met her soulmate, Qelbes, when she was still in her
mid-teens.
But her mother, my grandmother, was so concerned about the
fact that Qelbes was seven years older than her daughter that she
forbade her from seeing him.
Ever again.

Thankfully, eighteen years later, after my mum had dated a
parade of losers and spent eight long years as a single mother –

and Qelbes had suffered through a failed marriage – they found each other again.

The connection was real.
The spark was still there.
They had the wedding they'd always wanted and have been in love ever since.

'Also,' I could hear the gentle smile in my mother's voice, 'in the past, whatever I told you to do, and what you actually did bore little relation to each other.'
'So, whatever you decide, *filha*, I just want you to know that I love you.'

I let the movers know that my new address was in Double Bay.

6.

After completing my post-graduate studies at University of Technology Sydney (UTS) I'd immediately been offered a supply chain job at a major Australian health food and breakfast cereal company, based in Pagewood. A stone's throw from Sydney International Airport.

Then, not too long before I met Byron, I accepted a more senior role across the harbour, in Macquarie Park.

I was working for the largest food company in Australasia.

This is where I'd met Laura.

My colleagues were genuinely nice, all of them. Something few people can say.

But Laura was in a league of her own.

Super smart, hardworking and always generous – she used to bake me vegan treats even though she wasn't vegan herself.

Her Kiwi sense of humour was both silly and just a little bit dangerous, which I loved.

One day our department received a box of free samples, containing the company's latest line of healthy snacks.

We both took a bite, they tasted great.

Then Laura declared an eating competition.

What made this suggestion even more absurd is that we had just returned from lunch at the mall, where we'd both eaten oversized poke bowls.

But you couldn't say no to Laura.

Within ten minutes we were gagging and groaning, our bellies
painfully distended.
Faces covered in crumbs, saliva and tears.
We looked hysterical, but it hurt to laugh.
So gross, yet somehow glorious.

Laura's desk was right next to my own.
An egregious oversight by management, or a stroke of genius.
Who could say?
We made each other laugh throughout the day, but we also
worked hard.
There was no shortage of complex challenges for our busy
brains.

Our company produced dozens of healthy brands from hundreds
of product lines, sourcing thousands of fresh ingredients from
regional suppliers, working in partnership with tens of thousands
of retailers.
Our products were beloved by millions upon millions of loyal
customers.

Details within details.
A million pixelated data points in constant motion.
Laura and I were so deep in resource-planning software that
after a time it almost seemed like *The Matrix*.
I could predict how a fraction of a cent increase in the price of a
tonne of wheat in Western Australia and a surplus of cattle feed

on a dairy farm in Waikato would impact the delivery cost of a loaf of wholegrain bread in Port Moresby, Papua New Guinea.

Put simply: Laura and I crunched more numbers, did more data analysis, evaluated more risk, conformed to tougher regulatory compliance, and did more trend forecasting than any of Byron's banker friends.

Except we earned a fraction of what they did.

We put food on people's tables, they put money in their own pockets.
But who needs money when you have free snacks?

I loved my colleagues, enjoyed my work, and was proud of our company, especially after I stopped eating meat.
The majority of our popular food products were 100 per cent animal free.

But even before I met Laura, a workplace tragedy had set me on a different path.

David ran the breakfast cereal division, the biggest and most important division of our entire company.
He was almost twice my age, nearing retirement, but still passionate about his work.
Often working later than everybody else.

A true friend and mentor.
Always willing to take time out of his day to help teach newbies,
like me.

Everybody liked him.

One morning David wasn't in the office.
He was never late, so we all started asking the obvious
question.

Our fears were realised when we learned David had suffered a
severe stroke during the night.
He was in hospital.

Everybody at the office was very upset.
Someone suggested we all contribute a little money to send him
flowers.
Everyone agreed this was a good idea.
Then we went back to work, hoping for better news.

It never came.

David was still in hospital the following day, and we were told it
was unlikely he'd make a full recovery.

I asked around my colleagues and was surprised to learn that
nobody had plans to visit David.
'We're all slammed right now, and it's too far away,' I was told.
'The hospital is on the far side of the city. The better part of a
day to get there and back.'

So, I used a vacation day, and caught trains, ferries and buses till, some hours later, I reached the hospital, and was directed to David's room.

He looked different.
Deflated. Distant.
But still the man I knew well and owed so much.

David's wife was sitting beside him.
She was sad, but lovely.
Her eyes brightened as I entered the room.

I wanted to hug David, but I didn't.
We'd never hugged before at work and it seemed somehow disrespectful to start now.
I reached out to shake his hand but there was no strength left in his fingers.
So, I just held his hand for a while.

I passed along everyone's best wishes from work and told David how much he was missed. He nodded stiffly.
Then I shared the latest company gossip and he started to smile.

We talked.
It was difficult.
I had to be patient.

David's damaged brain was functioning at 50 per cent.
He needed extra time to comprehend what was being said.
Longer still to respond.

He spoke very slowly, and with great effort.
But he was present, and we talked.

When I finally got up to leave, I told David how much he meant
to me.
He had a tear in his eye. So did I.
Professional etiquette be damned.
I hugged David, and he hugged me back with all the strength he
had left.

At the office the next day, I told my colleagues and superiors
about David's condition.
The senior staff tilted their heads slightly to one side as they
expressed sympathy for David and praised me for going the
extra mile.
But no one else was prepared to visit David.
'It's too far, and I'm too busy.'
'He's getting excellent care.'
'He has his family with him.'

Out of sight, out of mind.

It rarely ever happens – just ask my mum – but I was totally
speechless.
I didn't know if this apparent heartlessness was professional,
personal, generational or cultural.
Were Brazilians and Australians so different?

Did the people in our lives cease to matter so easily?

I could not reconcile compassion and friendship being location-dependent.
The emotional delineation between work and home.

There are people you care about, and people you don't.
Spending time with people at work means you are sharing the bulk of your waking life with them.
A contract of humanity exists.

To suddenly stop caring about a friend and colleague, for any reason, is the same as if you never cared at all.

My corporate career had barely begun but I already knew that I could not, would not dedicate the best of myself to a roomful of drab office furniture, or a passing parade of indifferent executives.

If I did, what would be my living legacy – a faint impression of my bum in the cushion of my office chair?

Breath is finite.
This was my one and only life, and it needed to matter.
I was going to do something deeply personal with my remaining time on this planet.

And I already knew what it was.

5.

I love Natalie Portman.
At least to the degree that you can love someone you've never
met.
Maybe too much, perhaps not enough.

An incredibly gifted actor – *Black Swan*, *Closer* and *V for Vendetta*
are three of my favourite movies – but, more importantly,
Natalie Portman is a badass goddess.
Never afraid to speak up and say what she believes.
A tireless champion for women, for the oppressed, for animals.

I was at university in Porto Alegre when Natalie released her
limited-edition line of Té Casan vegan designer footwear.
Her beautiful shoes were never available in Brazil, but she'd
started something.
I could feel it.

Fast forward ten years.

Byron badly needed a new pair of shoes for work.

I promised him I'd find him a pair of non-leather shoes that
looked great with a suit.
Little did I know how hard this challenge would prove to be.

I was shocked at how few options there were.
Sure, if you wanted to chill by the beach, or become a hippie,
you were all set – moccasins and sandals galore.

And if you craved a pair of your great-grandfather's shoes that appeared to be made of cardboard, you were in luck.

My supply chain brain immediately identified a consumer need that wasn't being met.
A genuine business opportunity.
My heart told me this is what I'd been waiting for.

This was my moment.

The tiny fire that Natalie Portman had lit inside me grew and grew, until it consumed my fears, inadequacies, excuses and became my purpose.

I was going to create ethical fashion.

And by 'fashion' I meant stylish street shoes that were perfect for coffee or cocktails – gorgeous 'go anywhere' shoes.
And by 'ethical' I meant cruelty-free and zero waste.

To do this properly, a vegan commitment was just the beginning.
As a food industry supply chain professional, I knew all too well that roughly one-third of all food produced annually is wasted.

One out of every three bananas. In the bin.
Two out of every five loaves of bread. In the bin.

Almost three billion tonnes of food lies rotting on farms, is lost in production, goes unsold at supermarkets, or is left uneaten and thrown in the garbage.
Every. Single. Year.

One of the simplest ways to reduce waste is to reuse it.
I began researching new materials that would help remove toxic plastics from landfills and incineration stockpiles and prevent mountains of valuable plant matter from putrefying into unused compost.
It didn't take long.

Humans are amazing.

The creativity in this space inspired me.
Beautiful, hardwearing materials were being made from pineapple waste, recycled plastic, cork, cactus leaves and even apple peel.

I decided to name my ethical shoe brand No Saints.

None of us is perfect. I knew I wasn't.
And I had no right to judge anyone else for making choices different from mine.
I wasn't a fan of self-righteous cult-like vegan subgroups who wished harm on those who didn't share their extreme ideals.

I just wanted a kinder, healthier, happier planet.

Inclusivity was key to my business plan.
Creating shoes that everybody could enjoy wearing, whether they were Team Chickpea or Team Cheeseburger.

No virtue posturing.

My personal beliefs didn't make me better than anybody else.

If I was special in any way, it was in being prepared to act on what most people were already thinking: 'How can I look good and feel good while doing good?'

I knew this idea was bigger than me, but I kept my hubris in check.

Not for one second did I think No Saints could save the planet.

But I absolutely did believe, with every Brazilian fibre in my being, that if I worked hard, and enough people liked what I was doing, my ethical street shoes could be part of a movement to unfuck the world a little bit.

From then on, I spent every spare minute trying to turn my dream into reality.

Studying, planning, sketching.

Detailed notes on everything.

However, I'd be lying if I said I woke up every day thinking about ethical fashion.

I confess to having something else on my mind.

4.

When I opened my eyes each morning, my first thought was always how lucky I was to be with Byron.

This bed, this room, our home.
My cocoon of happiness.
Genuinely grateful.
A little love-smug.

Sometimes, I would just lie there for an indulgent minute or two.
Watching him sleep.
The rise and fall of his chest.
Luxuriating in the ease and surety of our intimacy.

But only sometimes.

Most mornings I would catapult out of bed at the sound of my alarm.
Early riser, go-getter, highly strung.
Guilty as charged.

Moving in with Byron proved to be even better than I'd imagined.
It took a little adjustment at first, but we were good together.
So good.

Byron liked to ease into the day like a hibernating bear in spring.
He enjoyed making fun of my frenetic morning routine.

By the time my drowsy lover remembered where he was, I was already pinballing around our apartment with the unpredictable angles of a trapped bat, dressing gown flapping behind me like a superhero's cape.

Byron enjoyed coffee like a normal person.
He poured it, drank it, and moved on with his life.
Not me.

Blame my Brazilian roots.

Look, if someone makes me a coffee it's just a delicious hot drink, for which I am very grateful.
But when I make it myself, it becomes a sacrament.

Every drop of dark nectar is sacred, down to the smallest puddle of dregs.

First, I'd prepare the precise blend of arabica and robusta beans.
Scalding hot water.
Carefully filtered.
A double dash of coconut sugar.
Then I would froth up almond milk with a fancy electric whisk and, oh-so gently, fold in this sweet, nutty cloud.
Exquisite.

Now it gets a little weird.

Instead of just drinking my precious coffee, I would sip-sip-sip away with the distracted air of a fickle hummingbird.
Flitting back and forth between tasks, making calls, texting Grace, doing my hair, putting on my face.

Reheating as needed, it could take me the better part of an hour to finish a single cup of coffee.
Sometimes longer.
And woe betide Byron should he attempt to put my unattended coffee cup in the dishwasher.

That's a mistake you only make once.

Morning beverage rituals aside, Byron and I cohabited famously.
Finding our rhythm came naturally.

We shared similar tastes and had the same circle of friends.
When we disagreed, we compromised.
If one of us needed space, we simply stayed out of each other's way.

When Byron had to work late, for example, I would spend more time on No Saints.
Perhaps go out for dinner with Grace or Olivia.
Margo, at a pinch.

Things were moving fast, but everything we loved about us as a couple was built on mutual respect as individuals.

Herbivore and omnivore.
Finance and fashion.
Night owl and early bird.

As Gilberto Gil famously sang, *'Cada macaco no seu galho'*.
'Each monkey to their own tree branch'.

We somehow knew how to make things work.
And we had fun doing it.

As a child, I grew up with animals.
Three dogs, one cat, two fish, two turtles and three mice.
But who's counting?

I loved being surrounded by life.
I wanted a home full of happy animals.

Byron loved this idea as well but pointed out that we both
travelled far too frequently to guarantee even the hardiest
houseplants the care and attention they deserved, let alone
emotionally intelligent pets.

He was right. Obviously.
But we both still wanted animals in our life.
So, I signed us up to a pet-sitting app.

Every now and then we'd pet-sit a dog while their owners were
away.
We kept the doggies feeling safe and loved, and they gave us our
puppy smooch fix for a day or three. Sometimes a month.
Win, win, win.

Our first year together was twelve crazy months of trying to make all our dreams come true at once.

To our credit, and amazement, we came pretty close.

3.

Double Bay is a beautiful and exclusive harbourside suburb.

Perhaps a little too exclusive. A little too ordered.
At times it looks like a parking lot for luxury cars.
A migratory gathering point for white, middle-aged lawyers.

We were both sick of paying rent.
We wanted a place all our own.
There was something to be said for less genteel neighbours.

And I missed the beach.

The Sydney housing market is a glamorous blood sport.

We were humbled a few times, but we kept our chins up and our
eyes open.
Within a month I'd tracked down the perfect Bondi apartment.
Clean and modern but not pretentiously austere.
Close to the beach, ocean views.
Natural light and fresh air flowed into every room.

I loved it.
Byron loved it.
We loved it.

A brief wringing of hands.

A few deep breaths.
And we were homeowners.

A place to nurture the hopes and dreams we shared.

The walk-in wardrobes in our new home were bigger than my
two previous bedrooms.
This extra space allowed me to have a proper home office.

With Byron's encouragement, I started developing my business
plan and product line for No Saints in earnest.

True love is having a partner who believes in you.

That winter we attended Grace and Colin's summer wedding at
the Palácio Estoril Hotel, on the Portuguese Riviera.

Such a beautiful couple.
Stunning location.

Happy tears.

Grace had become a sister to me.
We would laugh about how she had gone from being Byron's
friend to my bestie.
At the wedding Grace jokingly referred to Byron as my
'plus one'.

After the happy couple set off on their honeymoon, Byron and I
lingered in Lisbon.
We had special plans of our own.

First. Research.

Portugal's *sapateiros* are some of the best shoemakers in the world.
The craftsmanship of these traditional artisans is exceptional.
The gifted hands that execute every perfect cut and stitch are a
testament to almost fifty generations of skill and pride.
I wanted to visit their storied workshops to see if they would be
prepared to make shoes using Piñatex, AppleSkin and other
cutting-edge plant-leather materials.

I needed a No Saints manufacturing partner.
And I dearly wanted it to be here, with them.

Second. A meeting of even greater consequence.
It was time for Byron to meet my mum.

We boarded a plane to the Greek Islands.

2.

Juceli, my mum, and Qelbes, my delightfully goofy stepdad, had
laid a trap for Byron in Santorini.

We Brazilians are not known for containing our emotions.
And yet, when my parents welcomed us, they looked supremely
cool and calm in their Mediterranean holiday linen.
Chilled glasses of rosé loosely cradled in their non-dominant
hands.

But I knew better.

Brazilian Catholics don't fly halfway around the world to meet
the man their daughter is living with in sin without harbouring
some expectations.
And, probably, suppressing one or two deep-seated apostolic
fears.

As the sole bilingual, everyone looked to me to bridge the
language barrier.
Juceli and Qelbes both spoke a smattering of English.
The only Portuguese word that Byron understood was *caipirinha*.
Which he usually mispronounced.

I reluctantly accepted the unenviable role of translator for
conversations between my lover and my parents that were almost
entirely about me.
I was worried it would be extremely awkward for everyone.

But fortunately, they were very happy to talk about me as if I wasn't there.

It was mostly familiar territory.
General pleasantries, family health, the astonishing number of stray cats outside our hotel.

I wasn't expecting any great revelations.
Mum and I spoke on the phone more days than not.
I'd told her almost everything there was to know about Byron.
And Byron and I talked about my mum just as frequently, if not more.

It's not that we preferred to keep family secrets in the open, but our attitude towards personal information was decidedly clothing-optional.

Back and forth they went.
English, Portuguese.
Portuguese, English.
A friendly round of verbal tennis.
Albeit a lopsided match where one player was blissfully unaware that a far greater game was underway.

As both spectator and umpire, it was difficult for me to keep a straight face as Juceli expertly teased out Byron's intentions.
A masterclass in subtlety and focus.

When Byron confessed he was looking forward to marriage,
I gulped my rosé with as much dignity as I could muster.
Then, when he stated that he wanted four children,

I involuntarily clutched my womb, and a very small amount of
wine came out my nose.

Juceli just nodded and smiled and asked about his parents.
Her angelic demeanour never changed.
Qelbes beamed.
He'd been pried open so often by Juceli's tempered charm that
it was all but impossible for him to conceal his enjoyment at the
helplessness of others.
At the time of her choosing, my mum sent the men away on an
urgent and lengthy mission of little consequence.

There was women's business to attend to.

Once we were alone, she feinted with small talk about the
weather, Byron's height, and how tiny she felt next to him.
I was still reeling from the conjugal bombshell that had just been
dropped in my lap, but I knew her moves.

'Yes, Mãe – it's hot, he's tall, you're short. Let me have it,'
I demanded.

When she smiled this time, I saw all her teeth.

'Byron is going to ask you to marry him,' she announced.
Raising her glass in a toast to herself.
I responded with a loud, dismissive pish noise.
More wine left my face by accident.
Mum handed me a tissue.

'No. That's crazy – we've been together now for what, eleven months?' I asked.

'Almost a year,' she agreed.

'He's going to ask you to marry him, and he's going to do it here. In Greece!'

I shook my head and rolled my eyes.

But Mum knew my moves as well.

She just smiled at me until I couldn't hold it in any longer.

'Fine, yes,' I confessed. 'I've been thinking the same thing but was too afraid to admit it in case I was …' I paused, uncertain. 'Wrong.'

I took a deep breath.

'Byron is going to propose!'

We squeal-laugh-hugged so loudly that a mewling militia of stray cats flattened their ears and alarmed pigeons took flight throughout Greece.

From that moment on, my mother made sure her hair and make-up were picture-perfect, even while she slept.

Just in case there was any need to memorialise a special event with an official family portrait.

But there was no marriage proposal in Greece.

Any time Byron so much as looked in the window of a jewellery store my mum and I would clench our sacral chakras in excitement.

Regrettably, this happened quite a lot.

Byron had earlier expressed his desire to buy a duty-free Rolex. Only to repeatedly reconsider this purchase on the basis that we'd just bought a new home and conservative spending was prudent, if not mandatory.

As we said our farewells at Athens International Airport, Mum consoled me.
She argued that the admirable financial austerity that denied Byron a luxury watch had, likewise, justified Byron's decision to postpone the purchase of a diamond ring worthy of my love.
By her logic, the delay had only made our engagement more certain.
More magnificent.

But there was no marriage proposal in Brazil, either, when Byron and I joined Juceli and Qelbes for Christmas, in Caxias do Sul, later that year.

Or in Bahia, when we attended the most spectacular New Year's Eve party at Taípe beach.

'Don't worry, Lini,' said my mum, who was still ready for her close-up. 'When the time is right, it will happen. I know it. I feel it.'

I felt it too.

Which is to say, six months later I had a feeling that something very big was going to happen.

1.

The timing seemed perfect.

We were back in Europe.
More in love than ever.
Byron had become an uncle for the first time.

Marriage and children were creeping into conversations like angel's gossip.

I was excited for change.
I was ready.

Plus, all my hard work was paying off.
No Saints was building, taking shape.
I'd found business mentors and investors, eager to help.
Byron and I agreed it was time to quit my day job and start my company.

I'd already booked a booth at Vegan Fashion Week in Los Angeles to exhibit my first collection of shoes.
Byron's sister, Jackie, lived nearby, and had invited me to stay with her.

It was really happening.
All of it.

We flew to London to visit Byron's brother, Andrew, and his wife
Sara, and meet their beautiful baby daughter, Loulou.

Loulou was perfect in every way.
Soft skin, bright eyes.
Fine golden hair spun from fairy floss and moonlight.

I still found the idea of four mini-humans growing inside me and
violently exiting my body a tad confronting.
But I wasn't saying no to anything in this moment.
Every cell of my body was in love with this precious little girl.
I didn't want to give her back.

Following our swoony baby-fest in England, Byron and I met up
with JP and his gorgeous South African girlfriend, Emma, in
Dubrovnik.

JP looked so happy.
He confessed to Byron and me that he'd finally found 'The One'.

Love was in the air.
Our stars were aligning.

After Croatia, Byron and I spent a few wonderful days in
Budapest, before touching down in Spain.
A group of super-fun Brazilian friends we'd met in Trancoso
during our New Year's Eve celebrations were waiting for us in
Ibiza.

The EDM party capital of the world.

It was going to be amazing.

But first, Byron and I squeezed in a 24-hour stopover in my favourite European city, Barcelona.

So much to love in 'Barna'.
Art galleries, architecture and cuisine, the envy of the world.
The way the warm Balearic light accentuates the city's iconic floral motif in millions of panot street tiles.

I told Byron more than once that I would happily live here.
And I meant it.
Neither of us spoke Catalan or Spanish, but my garbled Portuñol would get us by.

Such a beautiful city.
So romantic.
So happy to be here with the man I loved.

A strange message was waiting for us at our hotel.
It was from my Aunt Jane.
The next day was her late son's birthday, my dear cousin Alexandre.

Alexandre and I had been very close as children.
Spending every summer playing on the beach together in Florianópolis.
We were both bookworms and had the same weird sense of humour.

We'd lost touch when we pursued different university degrees in different cities.

I'd studied engineering, while my cousin studied medicine and became a doctor, just like his mother.

Alexandre had grown into a remarkable young man, beloved and revered by all who knew him.

He'd become a psychiatrist and had dedicated his life to helping at-risk children and the unhoused in São Paulo.

Five years earlier, Alexandre had been driving back to Florianópolis for the holidays with his girlfriend and two colleagues.

It was a long journey, at least ten hours on the road, and his mother had begged him to fly home instead.

They were approaching the outskirts of Florianópolis, almost home, when a stray dog sprinted across the freeway right in front of their car.

Alexandre instinctively swerved to avoid hitting the terrified dog.

The car twisted off axis, tyres squealing, skidding, impossible to control.

They slammed into the guardrail and flipped over.

No one was injured except for my cousin, who died instantly.

Selfless to the end, Alexandre's final act was to save a little dog's life.

My aunt was very close to her son.

And their deep connection did not end with his death.

She wanted us to know that Alexandre had just visited her in a dream.

He kept calling out my name.

Again, and again.

He was desperate for her to warn me, or to look after me, or both.
It wasn't clear.

But it was clear was that Alexandre's ghost believed I was in
great peril.

Our last morning in Barcelona was busy.

We were up and out in the golden hour.
First, we found a cute little park by the water and did a light
workout to wake up our lazy holiday bones.
Byron teased me while I did a front plank, trying to make me
laugh so he could capture a funny video of me collapsing on my
face.
I didn't give him the satisfaction.

A quick shower at our hotel.
I slipped on a black and white cotton sundress.
Then we bagged up two weeks' worth of dirty clothes, which we
dropped off at a *lavanderia* a few blocks away.
They promised to have everything ready in time for us to pack
for our afternoon flight to Ibiza.

It was 9.30 am by now, and we were starving.
Our hotel was in La Barceloneta, but I knew a superb café on
the edge of El Born and the Gothic Quarter.
It wasn't easy to navigate the gorgeous maze of stone alleys,
medieval backstreets and hidden plazas.

But when we popped out at a pedestrian crossing on the bustling
Via Laietana, my breakfast bearings locked in.

A fight had broken out near the waterfront; a violent
disagreement between tourists and locals, perhaps rival soccer
fans.
Who knows?
The brawl was serious enough that someone had called the
police, and a Mossos d'Esquadra car was already racing to the
scene.
Full throttle.

Strangely, the speeding police car's siren was turned off.
Just flashing lights.
All but invisible in the bright morning sun.

The Via Laietana pedestrian crossing light turned green.
I stepped out onto the empty street.
Left foot.
Right foot.
Left––

Byron shouted my name.
Reaching out to pull me back.
But it was too late.

The police car had already taken me.

0.

Predator speed.
Running silent.
A killer whale in a crown of lights, rushing up from the abyss.
I was in its steel jaws before I even sensed its presence.

Bones twisted and crushed as my body was pushed through
itself, bent-broken over the police car's deforming grille and
bonnet.

My head smashed the windscreen into a cloud of diamonds.

The body that was once mine uncoupled from the earth.
Flesh and bone frisbee thrown 13 metres through the air.

The hideous wet crunch-thud of heavy impact.
Headfirst into a concrete gutter.

I lay on my back, fractured and twitching to stillness, like a
broken insect.

Blood-filled lungs heaving with effort.
Pulse flickering.
My shattered skull and ruptured brain spilling out every dream I
ever had onto the sun-warmed pavement.

I couldn't hear Byron screaming, 'No, no, no, no!'

Couldn't see him running, stumbling.
Dropping at my side.
The crowd of onlookers recoiling in horror.

Byron tried to staunch the bleeding. He failed.
His white t-shirt became a blood-soaked bandage.
Afraid to move me, but nonetheless gingerly tilting my head to
empty my mouth of blood so I wouldn't drown.
Byron stood up and screamed at the two stunned police officers,
my uniformed assailants, who were milling about in obvious
distress.
He order-begged them to call an ambulance. To do something,
anything, to help me.
Then, realising he was utterly helpless in the face of my
catastrophic injuries, he sat down beside me.
Shaking and crying until the ambulance arrived.

Thoughtful strangers came forward to silently hand Byron
my white Birkenstock sandals and phone, which the sickening
impact had thrown great distances in opposite directions.

No one found my favourite sunglasses, or any evidence that they
ever existed.

Paramedics appeared and took charge.
Byron was in shock, but they needed him to move out of the
way.
He rose unsteadily to his feet.
Dripping my blood and cerebrospinal fluid.

They gave him a towel to sit on in the front of the ambulance.

My sundress was cut away, I was carefully peeled off the
road, transferred to a gurney and locked into the back of the
ambulance.
Every second mattered, but they couldn't go anywhere until the
paramedics had stabilised me.
Nothing seemed to be working.

I was dying.

Left with no other option, they put me into a medically induced
coma and rushed to the nearest intensive care unit.

Joyless velocity.

Grim-faced doctors and nurses joined the paramedics in
formation as I was galloped into the emergency trauma unit and
put on life support.

Byron was turned away at the double doors and told to wait
downstairs.
He was shirtless now and had somehow lost his shoes.
A duty nurse, seeing a distressed half-naked man covered in
blood and gore, called for a doctor's assistance to diagnose his
injuries.

Once Byron's health, identity and situation were confirmed,
he was given a child's orange t-shirt to wear, despite being

two metres tall, and then led into a small room where he was surrounded by intimidating police officers.

They pressured him to sign legal documents written in Spanish. He refused.

Desperate for support of any kind, Byron called his parents in Australia, hoping for calming reassurances that no one was able to give.

Embeth and Mattys offered Byron what little consolation they could, while also preparing him for the worst.

Then they took charge of sending family reinforcements.

Andrew, Byron's brother in London, and Jackie, his sister in Los Angeles, were both summoned to Spain.

Byron had the presence of mind to text Juceli rather than call.

It was still early in Brazil. Very early.

Also, he was an emotional wreck and could barely keep it together.

He didn't want to panic my mother.

She panicked anyway.

Juceli called back immediately, first on my phone, then on Byron's.

Choking with emotion, Byron was unable to clearly explain, in English, what had happened to the only child of a distraught Portuguese-speaking mother in another time zone, recently jolted into consciousness by an urgent text message, hoping against hope for news of a marriage proposal.

Byron dialled Grace, in Sydney, connected her to the call, and asked her to translate everything he said.

My mum packed her bags in the dark and drove to the airport.

1.

A coma has two rooms.

The first is a padded cell in the belly of oblivion.
A dungeon of eternal night for the mind's eye.
Nothing comes in. Nothing goes out.
Memory and time do not exist here.
The ultimate oubliette.

The second room is far stranger.
A place of hunger and shadows.
The walls are porous, and every perforation is a tiny mouth, feeding on
fragments of light and noise, sensitive to scent and touch.
Your ancient animal self is chained here, snarling, weeping, vomiting
incoherent commands to your body.
Shrieking with pain.

2.

Mum arrived at the hospital as I was wheeled out of my first brain
surgery.

Just in time to be told that her daughter was going to die.

My head injury was severe.

On the Glasgow Coma Scale, from three to fifteen – with fifteen being normal or almost normal brain function, eight or less indicating a deep coma, and three being brain dead – I was a five.

I received the two extra points because the pupil in one eye reacted ever so slightly to light and noise.

A grain of sand tipping the scales of life and death.

I'd suffered a Grade 3 diffuse axonal injury.

My head had slammed into the police car windscreen so hard, the whip and twist of impact so great, that my brain had almost torn in half.

A third of my skull was cut away and placed in a refrigerated tissue bank for safekeeping.

Like my smashed arm and shoulder, my skull could only be surgically repaired if my cerebral oedema decreased, the intercranial pressure reduced to a safe level, and my internal bleeding had stopped … And I wasn't already dead.

I was given a 5 per cent chance of survival.

And if somehow, courtesy of a medical marvel, or by the grace of God, I lived, I would remain in a 'permanent vegetative state'.

Blind. Deaf. Mute.

No sense of smell or taste.

Unable to use my arms or walk.

My poor mother took the full weight of this.

It broke something inside her to hear it, and she wept openly, without shame.

But she was still standing and wasn't ready to give up on me.

She let the medical team know that her daughter was vegan, and to meal-plan accordingly.

Then she stayed by my bedside for six months and fifteen days.

3.

Cocooned in blood-soaked dressings and laced with tubes and wires, absurdly swollen and misshapen by the extreme violence I'd suffered.

Further disfigured by painful but non-life-threatening injuries.
Severe bruising, countless gashes and grazes, a fractured cheekbone, right eye goldfish-askew.
My toenails and toe tips sanded clean off against the grinding wheel of highspeed asphalt.

The name on my medical chart said Caroline.
But this wasn't me.
A hideously inflated and oozing red and purple likeness sculpted from chopped liver and clay.

Botero meets Hieronymus Bosch.

The intensive care unit was my home.
My whole world.
For a month and a day.

Vigilant machines and attentive medical staff made sure I remained technically alive.
Yet not quite alive.

My corporeal self was strapped to the bed.
A last-ditch attempt to tether me to the mortal realm.

The rest of me was treading the slackline between this dimension and the next.

4.

The human brain is a throbbing contradiction.

Fragile and robust. Brittle, yet soft and elastic.
A pitifully simple electrochemical battery and an impossibly complex and wondrous constellation of one hundred and eighty billion cells entwined in one hundred thousand miles of blood vessels.

The brain is our life-support system.
An organic vessel small enough to sit behind our eyes, yet large enough to house a lifetime of knowledge and memories.
A fathomless well of emotions, sensations and feelings.
A sleepless engine processing information and generating creativity.

Our mind, the invisible software of sentience, is programmed by the brain.
In essence, our brains define who we are, and how we see our world.

Whenever we speak in the first person, we are talking about our brain.
It is both the luminous seed and fertile soil needed to generate the
immeasurable potential that is to be alive and human.

And my brain had just been crushed by a two-tonne hammer.

Brain surgery is such an exalted profession that we never consider its
limitations until this esoteric specialty becomes a grim necessity.

With a traumatic brain injury like mine, neurosurgeons could do very little.
Relieve pressure, drain away blood and remove some clots.
Improving conditions for my brain to heal itself over time.

Or not.

Repairing damaged axons – the long, delicate nerve fibres that hardwire
the most sophisticated computer that has ever existed – remains an all
but impossible task.
Akin to knitting a shredded jellyfish back together with thick, crimson yarn.

From this point onward, everything depended on my brain's inherent
plasticity.
My neural network's ability to create new pathways around damaged
nerves and stodgy lesions, so that it could find a way to receive,
process, store and access information.

Would my battered grey matter restring itself with teeny-tiny lights, or
stay dark forever?
Impossible to know.

And there is no greater horror than the unknown.

5.

'For better or for worse.'
That's what they say.
Of course, no one ever reveals exactly how much worse.

Iron rusts. Gold melts. Diamonds chip and fracture.
Strength and beauty are constantly tested in this life.
For love, even true love, every day is a crucible.

My accident was a baptism of fire and blood for Byron.
To his credit, he stood tall.

Mum said he did everything you dream your soulmate would do, and more.
And she would know.

Byron became my mother's son-in-law in that hospital.
Putting his own pain and anguish aside, he protected me and helped my family.
Byron and my mum arranged shifts so that I was never left alone.

Not for a single minute.

Byron liaised with doctors and nurses, he dealt with the police investigation, he retained my lawyers, he organised Portuguese-speaking help and companionship for my mum.
He would tirelessly and generously arrange whatever was required to assist my recovery.
Day and night.

Byron would massage my hands and feet with my favourite cocoa butter.
He even changed my dirty adult nappy if the nurses were delayed.

True love.

Byron's goodwill extended beyond the confines of hospital.
His parents, Mattys and Embeth, and his two siblings, Jackie and Andrew, flew to Barcelona to comfort him, support my mother, and to offer me love and encouragement.

Andrew's sweet wife, Sara, brought a manicure set to trim and smooth my fingernails, which had become claws as I lay inert, swaddled in bandages.

Byron's friends and colleagues from Sydney, London and Singapore dropped everything to visit the hospital and offer assistance.

Our Brazilian friends that we'd missed in Ibiza, one of whom was also named Byron, came to Barcelona to spread good cheer in Portuguese, which gave my mum an enormous boost.

I couldn't know who was in my room and yet, at some level, somehow, I was aware of them.
Like a half-forgotten dream.

Mum would talk to me continuously.
Reassuring me.
Calming me.

She was a complete stranger to me then, as all people were.
And yet the powerful bond we share is such that I could sense her
presence before she even said a word.
Desperate to be close to her, but unable to connect consciously.
Unable to recall her face or speak her name.
I would writhe and groan in my bed, as if trying to give birth to the idea
of my mother.

Byron and our Brazilian friends would play my favourite songs out aloud
and even sing along.
'Shooting Stars' by Bag Raiders.
'Innerbloom' by Rüfüs Du Sol.
And finally, my absolute favourite.
'Roses' by The Chainsmokers.
Which Byron played three times in a row.

Say you'll never let me go.
Say you'll never let me go.

The family and friends who stood by my bedside during these darkest
days were, to me, celestial beings of light and love.

Utterly lost in a world of pain and confusion.
My only relief was hearing the voices of those I loved.
Their compassion and positive energy made an enormous difference.

My vital signs improved.
Intracranial pressure dropped below critical levels for the first time since
the accident.

I was detached from life-support and, to everyone's relief, my body took over, unassisted.
At last, I was wheeled away from the intensive care unit to the neurosurgical ward on the fifth floor.

It was finally safe to proceed with additional surgeries and scans.

My progress was slow but steady.
The bleeding inside my brain slowed.
Swelling receded.
My cerebrospinal fluid levels looked good.

The left hemisphere of my brain sustained the most damage, a region that is primarily responsible for speech, calculation and problem solving and controls all physical movement on the right side of my body.
For now, nothing on my right side moved.
Eyelid to big toe, still as stone.

But both hemispheres were where they should be.
They hadn't shifted during my 13-metre flight.
Most importantly, the brain stem itself seemed intact.

There was no guarantee that I would speak or walk again, but there was new hope that I might.
My left eye opened.
However briefly.

My mum smiled and wept.

$\Diamond$

FUNNY STORY

My family needed to unlock my iPhone to get in touch with friends and colleagues.
They also needed to access my luggage for clothes, toiletries and other essentials.

However, when they tried to use Face ID, my iPhone didn't recognise the brutally altered geometry of my battered features and the smartphone remained locked.

Then they found out that my suitcase was secured with a combination lock. A precaution I take when staying in hotels, no matter how nice they are.

No one knew the passwords except me, and I was in a coma.

Realising that I was unresponsive to verbal questions, Qelbes had an epiphany.
And I should mention my mum was not in the room when he had his great idea.

Qelbes took an oversized piece of paper and wrote in very large letters, all caps, 'WHAT IS YOUR PASSWORD?'

Then he showed this sign to me and eagerly held out a pen, as if I would read his question and neatly write the answer below.

Instead, I just lay there, doll-eyed, unresponsive as a lump of dough.
The hospital staff rolled their eyes and giggle-snorted.

Only Qelbes could make everyone laugh in such circumstances.

◇

One month later I was transferred to the prestigious Guttmann
Neurorehabilitation Institute.
Everyone was thrilled.

Until it all went wrong.

6.

At 6.30 am, following my first night in my new room at Guttmann, my
mum discovered that my pillow was wet with blood and ooze.

A doctor gravely examined my head and found that fluid was leaking
through my sutures.

Samples were collected.
The wound was cleaned and re-sutured.

At 6.30 am the next day, as soon as they would let her back in, Mum ran
to my room to check on me.
My pillow was soaking wet, slick and sticky with blood.

The doctor came again, and this time she was so concerned that she
asked my mum to wait outside.
Then she closed the door to speak privately with the chief neurosurgeon.

My lab samples tested positive for an infection.
A nightmare scenario.
An ambulance rushed me back to the intensive care unit at the hospital.

The bacterium in my wound was identified.
However, the CT scan was inconclusive.

The infection could be superficial, literally skin deep.
But if the infection had already penetrated my brain, all was lost.

COMPASSION FATIGUE

Everyone needs a guardian angel.
I had my mum.

She observed every single person who walked through the door of my
hospital room.
Most were selfless ambassadors of love and hope.
There were four nurses in particular – Maribel, Christina, Maria and
Bárbaro – whose kindness knew no limit.
Their warmth and consideration made every day a little brighter for
everyone they came in contact with.
Flowers bloomed in their wake.

But there were also others for whom subtle cruelty had become second
nature.

The Mossos d'Esquadra Major, Barcelona's Chief of Police, arrived
unannounced to look in on me, and pay his respects to my mother.
Instead of apologising, he informed my mum that his officers, the same
men who had broken her precious daughter and crushed her skull, were
in shock. Traumatised.
He then paused, as if expecting an apology from her.

A strange way to express his remorse.
Mum responded with a look of pained astonishment.

One afternoon, a very young nurse accidentally administered twice my prescribed dose of pain medication.
Thankfully Mum was watching closely, she saw my body become still, urine stopped dripping into my catheter drainage bag, my breathing become dangerously shallow. Then my blood pressure crashed.
Crying out for help, Mum explained what happened but, rather than admit her mistake, the nurse denied giving me any medication at all.
Doctors were called, quickly realised that my mum was telling the truth and were able to inject adrenalin to restore my blood pressure to a safe level.

After my head had been shaved for emergency brain surgery, following the discovery of the life-threatening infection, an irritated surgeon demanded Mum sign the release forms.
These documents granted formal permission for my skull to be reopened, and for skin to be harvested from my thigh if a graft was required to close the large wound on my head.
My poor mum, frightened, exhausted, and seeking reassurance, asked if this surgery was absolutely necessary.
To her horror, the agitated surgeon callously pantomimed ripping the forms in half and replied that she was happy to tear up the forms and let me die if that was my mother's preference – it was her choice.

This same surgeon later become enraged when she found me sitting on a sofa, instead of in my wheelchair.
She clearly had issues.

It's not my place to judge these people.
One can only imagine the trauma they'd been repeatedly subjected to for

them to feel it was preferable to play the victim than apologise, better to lie and risk a patient's life than take professional responsibility, easier to hurt others than be kind.

I can only think how fortunate I am to have a compassionate mother who was prepared to be my all-seeing protector.
My devoted human shield.

◇

I was wheeled out of the operating theatre at 5 am.
Mum was waiting for me, hoping for good news.

The infection had been successfully removed before it reached my brain.
I would have to remain in the hospital for an additional forty-five days and receive a hefty course of antibiotics.

The nightmare was over, for now.

While I slept a dreamless sleep in the recovery room, my mother went to the hospital chapel to pray and light a candle for me.
She was taking nothing for granted.

7.

Spain wanted me gone.

My three-month tourist visa expired while I was in a coma.
The international media coverage of my accident and the embarrassment

this had caused Barcelona meant that no one in government was doing me any favours.

The fact that I was bedridden, couldn't move or talk, half my skull was missing, my right side was paralysed, my left shoulder and arm were shattered, and I was being fed through a tube, did not apparently warrant any special consideration.

I was treated as though I had somehow insulted Spain's honour.
My mere existence, for all intents and purposes, was deemed unlawful.
Another arrow in my mother's heart.

There was a panicked and pleading scramble to secure a visa extension. The Ministry of the Interior refused to expedite anything, instead demanding countless documents, including bank statements and my original birth certificate.
My mum, Qelbes, Aunt Jane and Byron were all with me in Barcelona at this time, so it wasn't easy to secure these items from either Sydney or Caxias do Sul.

Grace helped translate key documents in Sydney for us but, in the end, though it cost her thousands, my Aunt Cátia personally collected and couriered all the original documents from Brazil.

At the eleventh hour my tourist visa was extended, and no one from the Spanish government tried to roll my hospital bed into the Mediterranean. Small mercies.

Mum was permitted to remain as my primary carer but, sadly, no such courtesy was extended to Byron and Qelbes.

They were required to leave Spain for no less than thirty days before they could re-enter the country.

My poor mother was alone again.
She continued to fight for a daughter who didn't recognise her or have any notion of the endless sacrifices she was making.

8.

The rough texture of the crisp, white hospital bedsheets against my bare skin.
The constant moaning and howling of damaged humans crying out in pain, in fear.

Linen and whale song.

I had no understanding of the eerie noises in the ward.
Of the noises emanating from my own throat.

When another patient would bellow or scream, my automatic response was to laugh hysterically.
A chimp on acid.

I'd like to think the staff had learned how to block out this asylum soundscape.
I can only imagine how deeply unsettling it must have been for my mother, and the loved ones of other patients.

◇

Wins and losses.

Byron phoned every day while we were apart.
His calls brought my mother relief, as much as they did me.
Mum would help bring the phone to my left hand and left ear as my head wobbled side to side.
I didn't understand a word, but Byron's voice calmed me.

I was finally stable enough for my broken arm to be operated on.
But the shattered humerus could only be rebuilt so much.

I now had a titanium shoulder.

Unconscious, semiconscious, I lashed out at the terrible pain.
My repaired left arm was locked down by my side, but I started whipping and slamming my paralysed right arm against the steel bed frame, like a bird of prey killing a snake.

The medical team worried that I'd damage myself further.
So, they strapped me into a restrictive vest, which I hated beyond words.

A surgeon injected Botox into my right arm to reduce the pain, relax the muscles and protect the nerves.

The Botox dose she gave me was so high that my right arm was limp for weeks, even after feeling returned.
I couldn't use either of my arms now, which was both frightening and upsetting, and delayed my rehabilitation.

My feeding tube was removed. So was my tracheostomy.
Liberating. Unnerving.
A medical conjuror pulling silk handkerchiefs out of my throat.

For the first time in months I was allowed to eat food normally.
But eating was no longer a natural feeling for me.
My jaw, mouth and tongue had become uncooperative.
Even with help, I struggled to chew and swallow and breathe.
If food slipped into my windpipe, there was a real danger of choking,
or developing a lung infection.

For a time, I refused to eat.
It felt wrong. Frightening. Unnecessary.
My weight dropped even more.
I became anaemic.

My doctors ordered a percutaneous endoscopic gastrostomy (PEG).
A flexible feeding tube that was pushed through an incision in my
abdominal wall, allowing food and, in my case, medicine to be delivered
directly into my stomach.

I fought the PEG at every meal and tried to stop people putting medicine
into it.
At some level it violated my sense of agency.

My right side slowly began to recover sensation.
Both eyelids were opening now, though not always at the same time.

I wasn't blind. Though I made little sense of what I saw.
I wasn't asleep. But not awake, either.

Remembered nothing.
Recognised no one.

I wasn't deaf.
I could hear ... sounds.
But words and music and the clatter of bedpans were indistinguishable to me.

I tried to talk.
Ever so softly. More breath than voice.
Lips barely moving but never still.
Endless whispered gibberish.

No one paid much attention to my repetitive murmuring until my aunt sensed I was speaking words, actual words.
But Cátia, who only spoke Portuguese, couldn't make them out.

She called my mum, who listened carefully.
Her eyes widened.
Mum confirmed Cátia's hunch with rapid nodding.
'Caroline is speaking English,' she said. 'Repeating two words, the same two words, over and over and over.'

A mumble-hushed recitation of my only memory of the accident.
An indelible snapshot, burned into a scrambled mind.
The exact instant when my head exploded.
'Broken glass. Broken glass. Broken glass. Broken glass. Broken glass. Broken glass. Broken glass ...'

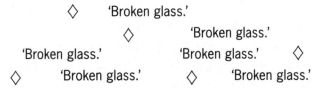

◇   'Broken glass.'
    ◇   'Broken glass.'
'Broken glass.'   'Broken glass.'   ◇
◇   'Broken glass.'   ◇   'Broken glass.'

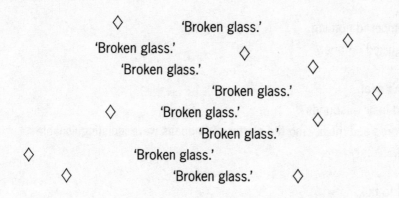

'Broken glass.'
'Broken glass.'
'Broken glass.'
'Broken glass.'
'Broken glass.'
'Broken glass.'
'Broken glass.'
'Broken glass.'

My mother suddenly realised I was reliving the horror again and again.
There was nothing she could do to free me.

She was inconsolable.

9.

Everything hurt.

Physical rehabilitation finally began in earnest at the Guttmann Institute.
Every part of my body felt alien to me.

I learned how to move my tongue.
My face. My lips.
My arms and legs.
Feet and toes.

Nothing was simple or came easily.
Even the smallest part of my body rejected control.
Fingers and thumbs were indifferent to each other.
Like asking five caterpillars to work together to pick up a spoon.

◇

There were two ongoing police actions related to my accident.
The driver who hit me was the subject of an internal affairs investigation by Unitat de Deontologia i Afers Interns (UDAI).

The UDAI found the driver not guilty of professional misconduct for failing to use a siren while driving to an emergency.
The siren is recommended practice but not mandatory.
He broke no law.

The reason for this was almost funny.
Barcelona's residents and business owners had been complaining of excessive police siren noise.
As a result, officers had stopped using their sirens in most situations, resulting in a quieter albeit more dangerous city.

The irony being that I was critically injured because the police officers were being extremely considerate, while racing to stop a fight, to prevent people from hurting each other.

We were told the UDAI investigation found the driver to be professionally negligent, for driving at a reckless speed with insufficient regard to public safety, and he was suspended from the force for twelve months, without pay.

The officer who hit me could be back behind the wheel of a police car before I learned how to walk and talk again.

But, as I say, that was just what we'd been told.
The UDAI investigation and disciplinary hearing were internal.

Behind closed doors.

We may never know if justice was served.

At the same time, the Guàrdia Urbana Accident Prevention and Investigation Unit (UIPA) were investigating the cause of the accident itself.

Their case was open and shut.

Byron's account was verified by five witnesses, the two young police officers in the speeding car and numerous traffic cameras.

The UIPA investigate any motor vehicle accident in the city of Barcelona resulting in injuries or fatalities.
Ten thousand per year, on average.

Their official investigation got underway while I lay bleeding on the pavement.

Officer Ágata, a UIPA agent, was at home when I was hit, enjoying her day off.
She saw my accident reported on the evening news.
The following morning, the UIPA agents assigned to my investigation asked for her help.

Ágata had lived in Boston for several years and, as the only English-speaking member of the UIPA, they needed her to explain to Byron what his rights were, what my rights were, how the department would support him and my family, and how the formal investigation would proceed.

When she first met Byron, Officer Ágata could see how devastated, confused and overwhelmed he was.
He was also, understandably, deeply cynical about police officers investigating police officers.

Ágata tried her best to help Byron understand what was going on and explain the UIPA's hard-won reputation for rigour and transparency.
She promised the investigation would be swift and thorough.

Then, when she saw me lying in the intensive care bed, something clicked inside her.

A connection formed.

Officer Ágata is almost exactly my height and weight, with long dark hair and olivine eyes.
There's a nine-year age difference, but the similarity is uncanny.
We could be sisters.

When she was eight years old, Ágata was hit by a car.

Her mother had given her money to go to the shop across the street, to buy sweets for her four-year-old brother.
Her mother and brother were waiting for her, on their side of the street, as she made the return crossing.

Her face was alight.
Candy squeezed tightly in one tiny fist, coins in the other.
The weightless feet and bright smile of a successful mission.

Ágata didn't look both ways before stepping out onto the street.
If her mother screamed, she didn't hear her.
Her small body skipping into the path of a family sedan.

The driver thought he'd hit a dog.

The base of Ágata's skull was fractured.
Her brain swollen.
Arm and collarbone broken.

She'd spent a month in intensive care, and a year in hospital.
In time she recovered and followed her dream to travel the world.
Nineteen years later she became a police officer who investigated traffic
accidents.

Officer Ágata's official duties were completed in a single visit.
But she felt compassion for Byron, all alone, drowning in grief.
And when she looked at me, she knew that I embodied her purpose.

She gave Byron and my mum her personal phone number, in case they
ever needed assistance, and promised to check in on me again.

Over the course of my hospitalisation in Spain, in three different medical
facilities, Ágata visited me more than eighty times.

One afternoon, at the Guttmann Institute, after my infection scare had
passed, Officer Ágata dropped by to see me, as she did several times
a week.
My eyes were open, but my mind was absent.
Body immobile.

After chatting with Mum and Byron, and wishing us all well, Ágata turned to leave.
At the door she instinctively turned back and gave me a quick wave goodbye.
I waved back.

Everybody gasped.

This was the first time I'd ever responded to a non-verbal communication gesture.

On weekends my mum would break me out of paper underwear prison.

She'd hire a wheelchair-accessible van and take me on field trips to restaurants and shopping malls.
A much-needed change of scenery.

It can't have been an easy outing.
Sometimes I would be happy and calm.
Sometimes I would scream and lash out violently.
When I tried to feed myself, I would end up with more food on my face and clothes than in my mouth.

People would stare.
Mum didn't care.

In her eyes, I could do no wrong.
I was alive. That was all that mattered.

I was doing my best to learn how to be human again.
While others were offended by my very public mistakes, my mum's eyes
shone with love and pride at my small victories.

At the end of our mother–daughter adventures, Mum wouldn't rush me
back to the hospital.
Instead, she'd take me back to her hotel room.
Let me sleep in a normal bed for as long as possible.
Keep me close.

I wasn't even aware that this beautiful woman was my mother.
But she never forgot I was her daughter.

Physiotherapy was getting harder.

I was learning how to stand up, inside a special safety frame.
My brain was so swollen and the intracranial pressure was so great that
when I was helped to my feet and the weight of my brain shifted from the
back of my skull to the base of my skull, I would immediately faint.

My body would sag into the safety frame, which stopped me from falling
in a heap on the floor.
When I came to, we tried again.
A little longer each day.

It was agony.

When my family tried to comfort me, I started crying.
And I didn't stop.
Couldn't stop.

During an exercise with alphabet tiles I tried to spell out the words
GO AWAY.

It wasn't clear if I wanted the rehab team to leave me alone, or if I wanted
them to help me escape.
I suspect both.

My aunt tried to encourage me.
'You are young, you are strong, you are going to make a full recovery, I
know it is hard but believe you can do this!'
I turned to her and, for the very first time, spoke clearly and loudly, in
perfect Portuguese.

'EU CONSIGO TUDO QUE EU QUERO.'
'I GET EVERYTHING I WANT.'

Qelbes and Byron returned from visa exile in time for Christmas.
Mum was overjoyed.
I didn't recognise either of them.
Yet I couldn't stop smiling when Byron walked into my room.
A fine golden thread tethered my man to my subconscious.

For some reason I started calling Byron, the nurses, literally everyone
Qelbes.
'Qelbes.'
'Qelbes.'
'Qelbes.'

Byron helped me put jigsaw puzzles together.
So many jigsaw puzzles.

I was pliant, not eager.

He'd take me for rolling-walks in my wheelchair to get fresh air.
Sometimes we'd watch old episodes of *Friends* together.

We even went out to a restaurant as a family.
Which was a special first, but probably not especially relaxing for anybody.

I kept losing my balance and made a terrible mess.
Also, no one ever knew what would come out of my mouth.
Half-chewed food, animal sounds, manic laughter, deeply personal
information.
Nothing was off the table.

A well-meaning waitress took pity on my shaved and battle-scarred head.
She told my mum that I reminded her of a slightly older version of her
son, who was twenty-two.
I startled the restaurant by blurting out that I was only twenty-one.
Which would have been true, eleven years earlier.

Everyone was too shocked to laugh.

On Christmas Day, Byron brought two bags filled with thoughtful gifts
from Grace, Olivia, Laura and Margo.
New pyjamas, comfy gym clothes, perfume, moisturiser, facial masks,
hair ties and even soft hairbrushes.
I was ecstatic.
Mum was in tears.

I still didn't know who my friends or family were, but I knew that I wanted
them all in my life, as much as possible.

10.

The new year did not start well.

Qelbes and Byron both had to return to their jobs.
They left.
Coronavirus arrived.

Mum joined the medical staff watching news reports in quiet horror, as
Covid-19 spread around the world.
Gradually, then suddenly.

Weekly pandemic updates became daily became hourly.
There was still no proven treatment plan.
No cure.
The death toll rose up like a tidal wave.

A sense of dread and urgency crept into the Guttmann Institute.
Everybody wanted me to go home as soon as possible.
My mother especially.

But I couldn't be moved until my skull was repaired.
And I was still too weak to survive the surgery.

I kept vomiting.
Accordion ribs, stomach cramps.

My mother worked closely with the nurses. They tried everything to help
me gain weight.

Every morning, without fail, Mum would bring me a freshly baked croissant and a coffee with almond milk.
This restarted my appetite.

Vegan desserts were the easiest for me to keep down.
So they fattened me up, one spoonful of fruit pudding at a time.

I finally began feeding myself with some success.
My right arm, though no longer completely numb and useless, had not yet fully recovered from the Botox injection.
And my recently repaired left arm was still very painful.
But I was determined to reclaim this responsibility.
It paid off.

A few weeks later Dr Gerardo Conesa Bertrán, the celebrated chief neurosurgeon, met with my mum.
She was able to sign the paperwork approving the reassembly of my cranial mosaic.

The roof of my skull was retrieved from the tissue bank and left to thaw.
For half a year it had sat on a dark shelf, frozen at minus eighty degrees Celsius.
Colder than the North Pole.
Colder than death itself.

Mum tried to stay calm as the orderlies took me away to the operating theatre.
Whether it went well or not, this would be my final brain surgery.

General anaesthesia causes serious damage to a badly injured brain.

The cocktail of anaesthetising drugs can reduce oxygen and increase carbon dioxide in the bloodstream, destabilising blood sugar levels, and increasing the pressure on the already dangerously swollen brain.

Each and every additional minute on the operating table can have devastating consequences.

To minimise the risks, Dr Bertrán personally led a team of his two best neurosurgeons.
The three of them working together as one.
Reducing an almost three-hour operation to less than sixty minutes.

A thirty-fingered maestro playing Prokofiev's impossible Piano Concerto No. 2.

Surgeons always look exhausted and rarely seem pleased when they walk out of an operating theatre.
It might even be something they practise in front of a mirror.

Thankfully the outcome seemed positive.

Dr Bertrán's team had succeeded where all the king's horses and all the king's men had failed.
They had put my shattered skull back together again.

Mum was told my recovery would be extremely delicate and closely monitored.
All she could do was wait.

And wait.

11.

We were running out of time.

My tourist visa extension had expired.
Once again, the Spanish government was demanding I leave the country.
Immediately.

Qelbes and Byron submitted a request for another tourist visa extension.
Dr Bertrán made it brutally clear to the Ministry of the Interior that if I
flew on a plane before I had stabilised, the change in pressure would kill
me.
I would be dead before the plane landed.

Nevertheless, the powers that be were unmoved.
My visa request was denied.

A death sentence.

When she heard the bad news, my mum was so distraught that she
tripped and fell in front of the hospital.
Fracturing her right leg, just below the knee.

A taxi driver rushed over to help her get back up.
At first, she was so focused on me that she didn't even notice the pain.
And later, when the knife-edged ache was impossible to ignore, she
refused to leave my side for medical treatment.

In desperation we reached out to the Brazilian Consulate.
They were happy to help, but their lawyer proposed a very different strategy.

Instead of seeking a second tourist visa extension, he filed a request for permanent residency.
This made no sense.
It represented the opposite of what both sides wanted.

I didn't want to live in Spain, and the Spanish government wanted me gone.
The sooner the better.

But it worked.
My execution was reprieved.

To celebrate my birthday, my stomach tube was removed.
And dozens of countries closed their borders.
Including Australia.

Coronavirus was galloping through Europe now.
Mum was terrified by what was transpiring in Italy.
A macabre parade of breathless bodies wheeled out of nursing homes.

It was only a matter of time before Spain suffered the same fate.

My traumatic brain injury and recent surgery put me in the highest risk category.
If I contracted Covid, the best-case scenario would be acute neuroinflammation that would likely reverse every hard-won gain made during my recovery so far, and inflict considerable damage on my central nervous system.

Death might well be preferable.

My mother was so frightened that she wasn't sleeping or eating properly
anymore.
She was losing weight at an alarming rate.
Her hair started to break. Then fall out.
The joints in her hands were seized and twisted with rheumatoid arthritis.

Spain's healthcare system knew what was coming.
They believed it was inevitable that hundreds of thousands, if not millions
of Spaniards would fall seriously ill.
And they were right.

Casualties doubled by the hour.
Extreme measures were being implemented to protect the most
vulnerable.
Including me.

The entire country started shutting down.
Doors and windows bolted.

My mother's hotel initiated an emergency closure, and she was forced to
sleep in a chair at the hospital.
Cafés and restaurants had shut their doors and sent staff home,
including the hospital cafeteria.
All Mum had to eat were my abandoned leftovers.

The Guttmann Institute was repurposed by El Sistema Nacional de Salud
to care for a massive influx of critical Covid cases.

All their neurorehabilitation patients were ordered to return to their homes immediately and self-isolate until further notice.

Without access to medical care, and no home to retreat to, Mum and I had nowhere to go and everything to fear.
New visa or not, we had to leave the country.

12.

Thirty days.

That was the absolute minimum amount of time following my brain surgery before I could be discharged from hospital and allowed to board a plane.

On the thirtieth day, exactly, Dr Bertrán personally conducted my final examination, supervised the new wound dressings and then, with reluctance, approved my discharge from the institute and authorised me to fly.

Byron had done everything humanly possible to get me home, quickly and safely.
But Australia's borders were shut even tighter than Spain's.
They didn't want me either.

Byron didn't give up.
He submitted request after request to the highest authorities to ensure

that I'd be allowed back into the country, and that my mum could accompany me.

There were virtually no international flights anymore.
The airline industry was all but grounded.
But Byron had found a plane flying from Barcelona to Sydney, via London and Singapore, and had purchased our tickets.
And not just for mum and me.
Also for a nurse and a paramedic we were legally required to travel with.

We arrived at Barcelona airport at 8 am, wearing protective masks and face shields.
Zero risks, zero mistakes. That was our goal.

But, despite our best efforts, things started going wrong almost immediately.

There was a problem with the nurse's visa.
Then the paramedic's visa had issues.
My visa wasn't even appearing in the system.
Mum called Byron in Sydney, and he sent it to her again via WhatsApp.

Then the customs staff identified problems with my medical documentation.
Specifically, Dr Bertrán's authorisation to fly.
We contacted the hospital.

At last, every crucial piece of paperwork was resubmitted, double-checked and approved.

Our bags were loaded onto the conveyor belt.

We were about to be waved through the security checkpoint when we were notified that Singapore has just closed its borders.

Our flight would not be able to land.

For the next hour and a half, Byron and mum looked for another way to get me home.

They explored all available options.

We had one chance.

Just one.

We could take a different connecting flight from Heathrow the following day, and still make it to Australia.

The only catch was that the airline stipulated that I would have to spend the night in a London hospital.

That was fine by us.

Reassuring, actually.

Mum readily agreed to this requirement and, finally, we were allowed to make our way to the departure lounge.

It was 3.30 pm. Our flight was ready to start boarding.

As we reached the departure lounge we were intercepted by airline staff who gave us the bad news.

England was now overwhelmed by Covid.

There were no available hospital beds in all of London.

We were not going to be allowed to board the plane.

They were already removing our luggage from the plane's cargo hold.

Oblivious and exhausted, I fell asleep.
My heavily bandaged head hung limply over my chest.

But my poor mother.
All alone.
Desperate to find a solution that didn't exist.

There were no other flights to be had.

Spain wanted us gone.
No one else would take us.
We couldn't even hole up in a tiny airport hotel room.
Every means of escape and place of sanctuary had been shuttered.

Mum began to weep.
Byron and Qelbes were calling her constantly.
But when they realised they were powerless to help, they wept with her.

At 5 pm our bags were returned to us.
We made our way to the only place that would grant us temporary
shelter.
The Guttmann Institute.

Right back where we started.

They gave us each a hospital bed and hot supper.
My mother's first proper meal in days.
We were grateful.
But we'd lost all hope.

13.

Qelbes hadn't given up.

First, he purchased all the remaining seats on the very last LATAM flight from Spain to Brazil.
The airline agreed to let us fly with them but insisted that I be accompanied by a nurse who spoke fluent Portuguese.

Qelbes then reached out to the Brazilian Consulate and begged them for help.
Amazingly, the consulate tracked down a Brazilian nurse who happened to be on vacation in Spain with her mother.
They were located just outside Barcelona.

Forty-eight hours later, the Brazilian Consulate sent two official cars to collect us from the Institute.
It seemed like an excessive gesture, but the emergency Covid rules decreed that there could only be one passenger per vehicle.

When we arrived at the airport, we were met by the nurse and her mother, who had also been chauffeured in an official limousine convoy.
It was like we were attending a royal wedding, or the Academy Awards.

We were welcomed warmly by a consulate representative.
He told us he had strict orders not to leave the airport until we were all safely onboard our flight.
And he meant it.

Everything was different this time.

We breezed through customs and airport security checkpoints, stopping only briefly on our way to the boarding gate, to receive one phone call from the Brazilian deputy consul general, and another from the director of LATAM Airlines.

Both gentlemen hoped we would enjoy a safe and comfortable flight and wanted to wish me a swift and successful recovery.

When we reached the departure lounge this time, my mother's eyes were filled with tears of joy and relief.
She had looked after me every hour of every day since I was injured.
Often entirely on her own.
Finally, someone was looking after her.

It was a beautiful moment.

I was an infant, drifting through the clouds.
Completely unaware of the devastating emotional toll my accident had taken on my mother, and everyone I loved.

Had I known that we were flying west, to South America, instead of east, to Australia, my heart would have ached for Byron.
The love of my life.
Sitting alone in our Bondi apartment.
Staring at the messages on his phone.
Just learning that I was not heading home to him.

Not knowing if I would ever come home to him.

14.

I can't recall how old I was when my mother told me her
story.
Our story.
For the first time.

It was, as with most stories about women and men, a
cautionary tale.

Juceli was just twenty-four years old, and not yet my mother.
She was working in Campo Grande as a dentist for the
Legislative Assembly of Mato Grosso do Sul.
Fresh out of university.
Her first job.

Young, lonely, naive, hungry, excited.
She was all of us in our twenties.

Juceli was living with her aunt and cousins at the time, just
until she could afford her own place.

Her eldest cousin, a lovely man, and my mother's most
trusted friend in Campo Grande, wanted to introduce her to
his buddy, Lars.
A handsome young farmer, the son of wealthy landowners
from Maracaju, two hours south of Campo Grande.
His family were soybean barons.

Juceli agreed to meet Lars.
She thought he was nice enough, but Lars was smitten.
As far as he was concerned, it was love at first sight.

Lars kept calling and calling my mother until she finally
agreed to go out with him.
He pursued her relentlessly.
Not the most creative strategy but, under the right
circumstances, an effective one.

It's hard not to be swayed by ceaseless adoration.

Juceli and Lars dated for the better part of a year.
Eight months.
Having fun.
Nothing too serious.
Until it was.

This was real after all.
Lars talked about forever and always.
They were meant to be.

And then, who knows what went wrong?
Love makes even the most sensible person joyously and
wildly irresponsible.
At least for a beautiful moment in time.

Juceli was pregnant.

She hadn't planned for this.
Her adult life had barely begun.
Just becoming the woman she wanted to be.

Lars didn't take the news well.
The same man who called all the time suddenly stopped
calling.
Stopped taking her calls.
Coward.

Desperate, frightened, unsure of everything, she approached
Lars' family for help.
They slammed their door in her tear-streaked face.
Instead of encouraging their son to do the right thing, they
advised him against it.
Juceli meant nothing to them, and whatever she was carrying
in her belly meant less than nothing.

She finally confronted Lars about the reality of her situation.
Their situation.
She needed him to be true to his word.
But despite what he'd told her repeatedly, Lars said he didn't
love her and he didn't want to marry her. Not anymore.
Then he sheepishly admitted he had another girlfriend.

She was also pregnant.

Juceli had to choose.
Between everything she'd dreamed of, everything she'd
planned to do, everything she'd worked so hard for.
… Or a daughter she'd never met.

She chose me.

Juceli knew the cost was great.
A baby could derail her fledgling career.
An anchor dragging behind her, slowing her down.
A child would also make it harder for her to find true love.
She would endure the stigma of being a single mother in a country with more judgemental Roman Catholics than any other nation on this earth.

My mother refused to be shamed into silence.
Rather than let people hold her back, she was determined to be unstoppable.

She knew that keeping me safe started even before I drew my first breath.
And that giving me everything I needed began by getting me what I deserved.
If nothing else, my biological father owed me legal recognition and child support.

Juceli took Lars' family to court.
And won.

She was determined to raise her daughter.
By herself.
She called me Caroline.

My name means strength.

15.

My mother spoiled me a little. Maybe a lot.
But she never pushed me.
She didn't have to.

I saw how hard she worked.

Mum was a voracious reader.

Her father had discouraged her from becoming a journalist,
but he couldn't extinguish her love of literature.

As a young girl, she read every single book her family
owned.
Then she walked over to their wealthy neighbours' house,
where they had a far bigger library, and read every book they
owned.

To no one's surprise, I was raised a bookworm.
By the time I was six I was reading three books a day.
I was precocious, and proud of it.

I would boldly debate and even publicly correct my teachers.
And if they argued the point, but were then proved wrong, I
demanded an apology.
Thankfully this cheeky behaviour made my teachers laugh.
Though it wasn't long before I was told to stop raising my
hand to answer every question posed to the class.
I didn't stop.

Mum was driven, and so was I.
I wanted to know and do everything.
In primary school, and then high school, I wouldn't
rest until my homework and study were complete to my
satisfaction.
Then I'd talk to my friends on the phone till midnight, or
until Mum caught me.

By 5 am I was awake.
Up early to wash, dry and straighten my hair.
Every single day.

I wasn't vain.
At least by Brazilian standards.

Rich or poor, personal appearance matters in Brazil.
Probably a little more than it should.
I wanted everything to be just so.

My mum called me her 'Little Perfectionist'.

The only things my mother denied me were sugar and candy.
As a dentist, she could not bring herself to let me eat
anything that would damage my teeth.
I like to think this was because she was also a perfectionist
in regard to her professional standards.
But I suspect it was also because I was the worst dental
patient she'd ever had.
I would wriggle, whine and squeal in her dentist's chair like a
puppy getting a vaccination.

Good grades and looking my best mattered to me.
Not because I was trying to impress others.
I was going places.

I set goals.
And I achieved them.

I wanted to build amazing things.
My heart was set on an engineering degree from one of the
best public universities in Brazil.
The application process was arduous.
An academic competition against 5000 other aspiring students.
We sat exams in Portuguese, mathematics, biology,
chemistry, physics, English and literature.

To be accepted by the university I needed to finish in the
top 800.
To be guaranteed a place in my preferred discipline, civil
engineering, I needed to finish in the top 150 candidates.

I finished in the top three.

My mum was thrilled for me.
I was so, so happy.
I couldn't wait to attend university in Porto Alegre.
Couldn't wait for the next chapter of my life to begin.

And yet ...
When the time came to leave home, I started packing my
suitcases in secret.
At night.

I was afraid that if Mum saw me getting ready to leave, it
would break her heart.
I already knew that being apart from her would break mine.

16.

I was made and remade in Brazil.

Our providential flight from Barcelona touched down in São
Paulo.
Mum took me straight to Valencis, a private clinic in
Curitiba.

I spent a month there, cared for by gifted therapists.

I'd been heavily sedated throughout my treatment in
Barcelona.
In Curitiba, my medications were drastically reduced.
My recovery accelerated.

It was at Valencis that I became aware of the passage of
time.

During a therapy session I asked my nurse what the date was
and found out it was late March.
This made no sense to me.

I'd departed Sydney for a spring holiday.
Yet, somehow, summer was over.
Flower buds were just opening, but now the leaves were
turning gold.

Christmas, New Year's Eve, my birthday.
The anniversaries of my first date with Byron and our first

kiss, first time we said 'I love you', the first night in our new home.
All gone by.

So many special moments passed while my eyes were closed.
Time and love and beauty lost, unrealised, beyond reach.
Flowers into smoke.

I suffered from anosognosia – completely oblivious of my traumatic brain injury – and couldn't begin to comprehend what had happened to me.
But in that crushing instant I understood something was very wrong.

So much of my life had simply slipped through my fingers, like forgotten dreams.
And, worst of all, I could sense how weakly I was holding on to whatever I had left.

At some deep level I knew the people in my life were moving on without me.
I felt dislocated from my own timeline.
Left behind. Abandoned.

I began crying.
Blubbery teenage heartbreak crying.
Small child lost at the mall crying.

Couldn't stop.

BREAKTHROUGH

I finally remembered my own mother.
Realisation dawned like the comfort of a warm blanket.

For the first time in half a year, I saw this incredible woman
beside me and knew her to be the mother who raised me
with love and strength.

She'd fed the furnace of my dreams.
Inspired, instructed and consoled me.
The source of my laughter, wiper of tears.
Devoted sculptress who'd shaped my face with kind words
and tender kisses.

Seven months, together-alone.
Reunited. At last.

From Curitiba, Mum and I flew to Caxias do Sul.
Qelbes was waiting for us at home.
Looking rather pleased with himself.

After considerable research, and at great expense, he'd
purchased a brand-new wheelchair for me.
It could be folded up and go anywhere.
Even in the shower.

I decided then and there, I was finished with wheelchairs.
I was going to walk again.

Starting now.

And that's exactly what I did.

Qelbes' face was somehow both crestfallen and delighted.

Which made me laugh.

It felt good to be home.

17.

CAXIAS DO SUL

I'd been away for so long.
Too long.
But you never forget your hometown.

Good memories and bad, it's in your blood forever.

I wasn't the first girl in our neighbourhood to suffer a
horrific brain injury.
Not even the first among my circle of friends.
And nowhere near the worst.

Two of my closest girlfriends had died when we were just
teenagers.

Rosana was a complicated but wonderful girl.
She came from a good home but had a difficult relationship
with her parents.
Her mental health deteriorated rapidly when she started
taking drugs.
After her father died of cancer, she struggled with
depression, started having suicidal thoughts.

When Rosana didn't secure a place at university in Porto
Alegre, she felt her friends had deserted her.

It was one wound too many, too deep.
She found her father's old pistol, went into a dark room and shot herself in the head.
I try not to think about Rosana's poor mum coming home and turning on the lights.

Felicia was a joy to be around.
Gifted in so many ways – everything she touched became a triumphant success.
She couldn't hide her genius; all witnessed her talents and were in awe.
Felicia was on the path to greatness, and everyone was happy for her.
One day she had a terrible headache, a migraine of sorts.
Her mother told her to come home for a day or two.

A short but well-deserved break from university.

Felicia's taxi pulled up to the house.
She stepped out of the car and fainted, her legs folding beneath her just a few metres from the front door.
A ruptured aneurysm.
She never woke up.

Barcelona wasn't even the first place where I'd been hit by a car.
Caxias do Sul held that honour as well.

When I was six years old, my cousins and I were riding a bike down a nearby hill.

It was Sunday afternoon, after church, around lunchtime.
The streets were virtually empty.
Fortunately for me.

When it was my turn, I pointed the front wheel downhill
and took off.
Halfway down the slope I'd picked up more than enough
speed and applied the brakes.
Nothing happened.

Nothing happened several more times before I reached the
bottom.

A white taxi had just pulled over to collect a passenger.
The car was slowly rolling away as I zoomed in front.
The taxi collected me as well.

I was knocked senseless for a few seconds, then came
rushing straight back to the land of the living.
Wide-eyed and confused.

I kept asking what day it was, what time it was, and what
happened.
I was still asking those same questions, on a loop, inside the
ambulance.
Inside the hospital.

I had no memory of the accident.
But other than a mild concussion, I suffered no serious
injuries.
Thankfully the taxi had barely reached twenty kilometres
per hour when we'd collided.

The doctor recommended that I remain in hospital, under observation.
But my mum wanted me back home.
Where she could keep me close and take care of me.
All night.

She watched over me as I slept.
Gently slapping my little hand away when I started twisting my hair around my fingers so tightly that the fine brown strands started breaking.
Something I'd done since I was a baby.

By the following morning the fuzzy events leading up to, but not including the actual crash, were back in focus.
But even as I was recovering my memory, I had my wits about me.
I seized the moment to beg my mum for a puppy.

We adopted a white toy poodle named Toby.

'*Eu consigo tudo que eu quero.*'
'*I get everything I want.*'

But what I wanted now, thinking of dear Rosana and Felicia, was to be the girl who lived.

18.

I knew where I was.
Totally aware that I was in Brazil.
Just didn't know why.

My past and present were an aching blur.
But the people who were important to me, slowly came into focus.

I knew Qelbes.
Remembered him.

I had known him since I was seven.
Qelbes moved in with us when I was eight.
He became more a friend and playmate than a stepfather.

A wonderful cheerleader.
Always joking, always laughing, always kind.

I missed Byron.

My whole heart missed him.
I remembered how much I loved him.
And how much he loved me.

And I also remembered our close friends in Sydney.
I was excited to see them again.
Even Margo.

I felt ready for the world, but I wasn't.

Not a functioning adult human by any means.
Naive, oblivious and volatile.

More adept at conversation than, say, a howler monkey.
More credulous and unstable than, say, a child actor.

It took a compassionate army of physicians, therapists and a
tireless mother to ensure I made incremental progress.

I was walking everywhere now.

But my gait was ungainly.
Jerky steps, upper torso twisted strangely.
Slack-faced. Eyes glazed.
A zombie with great legs.

Words were getting through to my brain on a more
consistent basis.

I started responding.
But when I opened my mouth to speak, I would be greeted
with tight awkward smiles and anxious, pitying nods.
No one could understand me.

I still had absolutely no idea I'd been hit by a car.
To be honest, I thought I was fine.
Most of the time.

I didn't really understand numbers anymore, or money.
Odd for someone who deadlifted massive budgets and
performed mathematic wizardry for a living.

The pitiful compensation from Spain arrived in my bank
account.

When it was converted from Euros into Brazilian Reais, at
an exchange rate of five to one, I thought I was a millionaire.
Set for life.

In fact, I didn't receive enough money to cover more than a
few years of physiotherapy and groceries.
But, through the kaleidoscopic lens of my fractured brain,
the numbers dazzled me.

When Mum and I walked around town, I would offer to give
her whatever was on display in the storefront windows.
'Do you like that?' I would ask excitedly. 'I can buy it for
you!'

My clear-eyed mother, who understood my financial peril,
didn't know whether to laugh or cry.

Sometimes she did both.

◊

My brain had been reset.
English was now my default language.

This happens sometimes with traumatic brain injuries.
I've heard of people who've woken up from a coma speaking
a new language they'd never spoken before.

I was diagnosed with Wernicke's aphasia, a language and
comprehension disorder resulting from the left hemisphere
of my brain being pounded into sausage meat.

When people spoke to me at normal speed their words
seemed random and confusing.
Information quickly overwhelmed me.

Took a minute, maybe more, to process what I was being told.

And if more than one person was talking at a time, I was
lost.

So lost.
Like watching a foreign movie that you didn't know was a
musical.
Suddenly people are singing, everyone is singing at you, and
you have no idea what the hell is going on.

And then, when I tried to speak, thoughts and words
tumbled around in my head like overexcited marbles.
I could never be entirely sure what was going to spill out of
my mouth.

Possibly subject and predicate, mumbled back to front.
Or something as unintelligible as wind chimes.

It slowly dawned on me that I was struggling to be
understood.

I didn't know what the problem was.
But at some level I grasped the idea that my cerebral
dictionary contained very few intelligible words.
In English or Portuguese.

Having successfully self-diagnosed, I prescribed myself a
course of vintage American sitcoms.
I started re-watching old episodes of *Friends* on my iPad.

I'd listen carefully to their cheesy-snappy-funny dialogue.
Then I'd pause the show, write down what they'd just said, as
best I could.
Speak the lines aloud to myself.
Press play. Watch and transcribe the next scene.
Repeat the exercise.

Some parents would think their former academic star was
completely washed up if she spent all day watching the
whitest television comedy from the 1990s.
But Mum saw exactly what I was trying to do.

I was the star pupil at an exclusive *Friends* Language School.
And I was going to get straight As or die trying.

My mother picked up on other small improvements
that most people might have missed, or completely
misunderstood.

Back at Valencis, Mum noticed that I was looking at myself
in the mirror.
I seemed concerned.
Mum realised that, for the first time in a year, I was
becoming self-conscious about my appearance.
My brown hair was slowly and unevenly growing back after
being shaved multiple times in hospital.
I was regaining degrees of self-awareness.
My mum wanted to celebrate and nurture this.

Make-up and personal grooming lessons were just the
beginning.
Mum innately understood that, just like turning up late to
everything, big hair is a Brazilian woman's birthright.

She knew exactly what to do.

Mum tracked down a great hairdresser who put in killer hair
extensions.
When I looked in the mirror again.

Boom.

As far as I was concerned, I was back, baby.

19.

I love my family, I love my culture, I love my country.
And yet, my passionate connection with Brazil is, was,
well … complicated.
There were times when I preferred a long-distance
relationship.

Let me explain.

FIVE ROBBERIES

I was walking home from high school with a girlfriend when
my sunglasses were stolen.
Snatched right off my head in broad daylight by a man
riding past on a bicycle.
Not the end of the world, sure.
But we didn't have a lot of money, I didn't have another pair,
and this really stung.

My university classmates and I were sipping strawberry
daquiris at a local bar when my handbag was stolen.
We weren't naive.
We'd placed our bags on the table, keeping them right in
front of us.
But the sneaky thief was watching us the whole time.

Waiting for a split second when we were distracted to make their move.

My whole life was in that bag.

A friend dropped me home in Porto Alegre one evening, following a late afternoon lecture at university.

He found a perfect parking space, right in front of my apartment building.
I thanked him and opened the door to leave but he launched into a long, awkward conversation about how friendships can evolve over time … etc.
Specifically, he wanted me to take his virginity.

Look, he was a nice guy, but just a friend. Period.
So, I was trying to say 'no way' without hurting his feelings, when two men with guns told us both to get out of the car and leave everything of value inside.

They stole his car, a brand-new white VW.
They also took our phones, my engineering textbooks and my friend's Nike sneakers.
He gave his statement to the police wearing socks.

Good news, his car was recovered a few days later.
Bad news, it was soon stolen again.

To pay my way while I was at uni, I landed a day job with a direct marketing advertising agency.

One Friday, I dropped in on one of my clients, a travel agency, to finalise a project before they shut down for the 'Day of the Dead' long weekend.
When I arrived at their office I was met at the door by a gun-waving junkie.
He dragged me inside and told me to get down on the floor.

Inside, the entire staff, a dozen employees, were already seated, slumped over on the carpet.
Many of them were in tears.
A second junkie was storming around the office, crazy-eyed, whisper-shouting at everybody to put their handbags, wallets and valuables on the floor in front of them, as well as their car keys.
Both robbers were high on crack cocaine.

Terrifying. Obviously.

Be that as it may, I had a brand-new handbag that I absolutely loved.
So, I quickly dumped everything out onto the floor; lipstick, eyeliner, chewing gum, a bag of snacks, random receipts and my company laptop.

I even scattered some $10 Real bills on top, to make the robbers think they had my money.
But I kept my wallet and phone inside my precious handbag.

Then I tried to hide my handbag by pressing it against my belly and hunching over.
Like I had terrible gas.

When the junkies ordered us to move into the conference room, I was eager to get inside, where I quickly tossed my handbag behind a chest of drawers.
After muttering various threats, the junkies locked everyone into the conference room and then made their escape.
Once we were certain they'd left the building, I recovered my handbag and called the police to come and rescue us.

The additional bonus, for me at least, was that the junkies escaped in someone else's car that was, no doubt, far more luxurious than mine.
They left the keys to my unwashed, second-hand Fiat Punto lying on the floor.
Not a huge surprise, but still ... winning.

My mum and I were robbed in the street, while walking to a private sports club with a swimming pool.

I was home for my summer break and begged her to take me there.
In Porto Alegre I was at work by 6 am and didn't get home till the early evening.
Then I'd quickly eat, shower and change my clothes, before racing over to the university to attend night classes till 10.30 pm.

Desperately needed some sun.

We'd parked adjacent to the club's entrance and were
crossing the street when two young men approached us.
I was wearing a hot pink bikini, white short-shorts and
bright white Havaianas.
Mum looked amazing in her black bikini and miniskirt.

For a second, we thought the creeps were just checking us
out.
I was waiting for them to hiss and leer at us, perhaps waggle
their tongues a bit.
Classic entry-level Brazilian catcalling.
They pulled out handguns instead.

Mum was furious.

She knew they wanted to steal her new convertible, and she
wanted these punks to know she wasn't afraid of them.
But her defiance enraged and emboldened the two thugs.
In response, one robber put his pistol to my head.
The gun barrel pressed hard against my temple, creating a
circular indentation in my skin.

Mum looked across in horror. Saw my face turn pale, my
features slacken.
Fear-induced catatonic stupor.
Warm urine gushing down my legs and splashing over my
white sandals.

Mum told the robbers that if they took the gun away from
my head, they were welcome to take whatever they wanted.

Her handbag, her wallet, cash, credit cards and chequebook.
Our phones.
Her car with everything in it.
Even the Paulo Gustavo DVD sitting on the back seat –
Mum's favourite comedian.

They took it all.

I don't remember how long I stayed locked inside my
one-person prison of terror, but I know that Qelbes took us
home.

The two thieves drove Mum's convertible as far as they
could before abandoning it with an empty petrol tank.
It was found at the side of the road, deep inside the
rainforest.
Thankfully, it was still in perfect condition when the police
recovered it.
Not a scratch.

But the robbers kept Mum's Paulo Gustavo DVD.

20.

Byron couldn't visit me in Brazil, due to strict Covid lockdown policies.
But he sent me flowers, cards and chocolates.
And so much more.

He called me every single day from Bondi.
Just like he had when I was in the hospital in Barcelona, eight months earlier.

When we talked, Byron would say beautiful and loving things to me.
I would babble and chatter away like a happy baby, or an overstimulated budgerigar.
Perhaps only one out of every four words that came out of my mouth made any sense.
But I knew what I felt and what I was trying to say.

So did Byron.

Byron had given me a beautiful pink journal while I was in hospital.
'ALL YOU NEED IS LOVE' was written across the front cover.
Inside, he had written a long love letter.
He had also drawn sweet pictures alongside rehabilitation

activities, word exercises and silly little games we'd played together, like tic-tac-toe.

This journal became my bible while I was in Caxias do Sul.

Byron signed off his love letter with a massive I ♥ U.
Next to this, he'd written my full name, date of birth and our Bondi home address.
To help me remember exactly who I was, and where I truly belonged.

Hearts, hearts, hearts.
Byron had drawn so many in the journal.
Some contained our names, others our initials.

Countless tiny hearts were shown filling up a glass vase, on which he'd written, 'Every Morning Is A Gift', in Catalan.
I assumed a nurse helped translate this for him, probably Maribel.

I would practise my writing by copying his little love notes in my chaotic scribble.

> **Dear Caroline**
> **You are the most important**
> **person in the whole world.**
> **I love you so much!**
>
> **I love you more each day.**
> **Love Byron**

Another one in all caps.

BYRON

LOVES

CAROLINE

FOREVER !!

♥ ♥ ♥

♥ ♥ ♥

In the hospital Byron had traced our left hands, side by side,
over two pages.
He'd made his fingernails pink, and had drawn a big, shiny
engagement ring on my ring finger, using coloured pencils.
The band was blue.
The sparkling diamond, yellow.

I stared and stared at this picture.
Day after day. Again and again.

Couldn't wait for us to be married.
I started planning our Australian wedding from Brazil.
I sent Byron photographs of every bridal gown that I liked.

He loved them all.

I didn't think I could love Byron any more than I already
did.

But then his amazing friends JP and Emma set up a GoFundMe page in Australia, to help my mum recover some of the not-so-small fortune she and Qelbes had been forced to spend because of my accident.
Travelling back and forth to Spain, staying in hotels, and countless other major expenses.
To stay by my side, Mum had been forced to shut down her dental practice completely.

Qelbes also took a lot of time away from the insurance business he'd built over thirty years.
He'd recently ordered a new car and, by coincidence, the delivery date was the day after my accident.

Instead of driving home in a new vehicle, he asked the car dealer to cancel his order and refund his money.
Qelbes was afraid we would need every penny to help cover my medical expenses.

He was not wrong.

The GoFundMe page raised over sixty thousand Australian dollars.
More than two hundred thousand Brazilian Reais.

If anyone imagined my mum was all cried out, they were sorely mistaken.

Physical therapy hurt so badly that I couldn't sleep.
Speech therapy was both frustrating and exhausting.

I had quite a few meltdowns while I was staying with my parents.

I don't know how they put up with me.
But I do know how I kept going.

Byron and I were sending countless little messages and pictures back and forth via Instagram and WhatsApp.
Even on the hardest days, these tiny love bombs boosted my spirits.

I loved that Byron would always include me when he was out with our friends, by sending photos of whatever they were doing.
These little windows into our former life made our time apart bearable.
Also slightly more painful.

He would thrill me with uplifting video messages.
Some were montages of our most fun and romantic moments, set to my favourite music.
In others, he'd take me on tours of our apartment in Bondi.

He'd show me my home office, ready for me to get back to work.
My walk-in wardrobe, with all my clothes and jewellery.
Everything waiting for me to come home and reclaim what was mine.

The bed where we made love.

Byron sent me a sweet Valentine's Day gift with a beautiful message.
But, with the world in Covid chaos, it didn't arrive in Caxias do Sul until mid-June.

> **To my beautiful Caroline, happy**
> **Valentine's Day! I love you so**
> **much and I'm so incredibly proud**
> **of how well you are recovering.**
> **Please keep on fighting. I love**
> **you and can't wait to see you in**
> **Brazil!**
>
> **Byron** ♥

July and August came and went.
Byron never arrived.

Australia had banned citizens from leaving the country back in March.

I reached a tipping point.

I wanted, I needed to return to Bondi.
It's all I talked about with Mum.

I couldn't stand being apart from Byron any longer.
Couldn't reconcile being on the opposite side of the world.

My recovery slowed.
I became depressed.

Even my mum, who would rather I never left home ever
again, knew it was time for me to return to Sydney.
As always, she put my happiness first.

There was only one problem.
Getting into Australia was impossible.

21.

Australia had locked its borders and thrown the key into the sea.
Nobody was going in or out.

Of course, no one else had a lover like Byron, or a best friend like Grace.

Byron submitted form after form.
Letter after letter.
Seeking, begging, demanding permission for me to come home to him in Bondi.

Grace translated countless documents from Portuguese to English and back again.

Australia is famous for many things but, historically at least, welcoming foreigners to their golden shores isn't exactly one of them.
Understandably, the coronavirus pandemic hadn't softened this attitude.
Australia is a difficult place to secure a permanent resident visa, even at the best of times.
It's even more difficult to become a citizen, as I could attest – I'd submitted my naturalisation paperwork as soon as I was eligible.

To be fair, there are many places that are harder still.
Bhutan, Vatican City and the Moon. To name a few.
Was Australia even worth all this trouble?

Yes.

To me, it absolutely was.
This beautiful country was my adopted home.
This is where my closest friends were.

This is where I lived with the man I loved.

The Australian government finally agreed that I was entitled
to return home.
As a resident taxpayer, my right to access vital public health
services that I desperately needed was irrefutable.
But they still tried to smother our request in tedious
paperwork.
However, for two spreadsheet-devouring bankers like Byron
and Grace, this was just another morning at the office.

Even having approved my return, the government made my
family and me jump through a carnival of medical hoops.
But, again, after what we'd endured in Barcelona, we barely
blinked at this.

Qelbes started looking for flights.

Our departure date was drawing near.

I was counting down the days, the hours when I received an anonymous message via Instagram.

> **Caroline, Byron is a lying, cheating prick. We've been together and ducking* for 8 months.**
>
> **Fucking***

There were also two photos attached.
But they were black-blurred out and marked as sensitive content.
I didn't understand what I was looking at, I didn't know how to reveal the photos.

Instead, I sent everything to Byron.

He assured me this was just malicious spam.
Someone was probably trying to phish me.
'You should just ignore it,' he said.

22.

We tested for Covid.
Then we tested again.
We boarded our first flight on 5 September.

Normally, when travelling to Australia from Brazil, you head
west.
Santiago, Chile, then Auckland, New Zealand.
Crossing the Pacific and touching down in Sydney, twenty-
four hours later.

However, Covid-19 travel restrictions ruled out a normal
flight plan.

Our only option was to fly east from São Paulo to Doha, in
Qatar, and then take a direct flight to Sydney from there.
The Atlantic Ocean, then the Indian Ocean.
Twice the distance, twice the time.

My freshly knitted skull felt every one of those forty hours
in the air.

In the first twelve months of the coronavirus pandemic, no
government on earth knew what to do.
There were no vaccines, no proven treatments.

Medical science was still playing catch-up.
No one was learning from each other's mistakes.

Misinformation ran rampant.

Some public health measures were overkill.
Others fell short.
Some achieved too little too late.

Australia was no different.

Despite being one of the world's healthiest countries, the pandemic wasn't handled much better here than anywhere else.
Aussie health officials instigated tough and lengthy lockdowns to compensate for a lack of preparedness and a delayed vaccine rollout.
It wasn't pretty.

The one major advantage, being an island nation surrounded by sea turtles, was geographical isolation.
Like Japan and New Zealand, Australia's closed borders were far more effective at delaying and reducing exposure to the deadly virus.

Which was why they weren't taking any chances at Sydney airport.

We hobbled off our second marathon flight, still wearing our Covid masks and face shields.

Almost immediately, we hit an intimidating dark blue wall of
Australian Border Force officers.
They made it clear that Australia wasn't open to visitors.

The Department of Home Affairs was not authorising entry
for any foreign nationals.

A Portuguese-speaking customs official was brought over.
A great relief, as Qelbes and my mum did not speak fluent
English.
And I didn't speak fluent anything anymore.

A lengthy conversation ensued.
The officers wanted to know how we'd even got on the plane,
let alone dared to set our Brazilian feet down on Australia's
golden soil.

After checking the validity of our passports and visas they
declared that only I could enter the country.
My parents would have to return to Brazil, without leaving
the airport.

Fending for myself was not a situation any of us wished to
contemplate.
My mother's face completely drained of colour.
But she called their bluff.

Thanks to Byron and Grace, our paperwork was in perfect
order.
The customs officials double-checked everything and,
finding no legal basis to detain us, stamped our documents,
approving entry to Australia.

After passing another Covid test, we were herded onto
a bus that would take us to our mandatory quarantine
accommodation.

No one told us where we were headed.
Which felt both rude and unsettling.

But, in the end, it took more time to load and unload the
bus than it did to reach our destination.
So, we were still in Mascot, or very close by.
Not far from where I used to live when I worked in
Pagewood.

23.

Somehow, all our luggage was lost during the five-minute bus ride from the airport.

The quarantine hotel check-in process was memorable, if only because it ended with us being locked inside our room.

Two police vehicles were stationed outside the building to prevent illegal departures and recapture extreme sleepwalkers.
I didn't know why, but I felt uncomfortable seeing them parked there, day and night.

Our quarantine apartment was basic, but comfortable.
Neither the Ritz, nor a Soviet Gulag.
Though perhaps not the hotel where we three would have chosen to spend 360 consecutive hours together.

It was unseasonably cold when we arrived. And raining.
We enjoyed uniformly bleak views of wet concrete from every window.
A far cry from my sunny memories of Australia.
I could only imagine what my mum and Qelbes thought.

That evening, Byron and JP arrived to welcome us.
Grace and Olivia came by later as well.
The police made sure they didn't enter the building.
They shouted happy greetings from the street below.

I was fat-puppy-at-dinnertime excited by the mere sight of
them.

Byron sent up an expensive bottle of champagne, local
Aussie delicacies, a beautiful pair of new shoes, and a very
romantic card.
The girls sent up a gorgeous welcome package.
Balloons, flowers, a plush koala, vegan chocolates galore.
And a sweet note from all my friends.

> Dear Caroline,
> Welcome Home!
> We are so happy to have you
> back in Sydney. We can't tell you
> how proud we are of you and your
> recovery and progress so far. We are
> so sure that you are only going to
> continue to get better and we are
> here to support you in every possible
> way. We have missed you so much
> and can't wait to see you!!!!!!
> All our love,
> Your Sydney Friends
>
> Xxxxxxx

◇

I was deeply touched.
But also puzzled.

The reference to my ongoing recovery and progress
confused me.
No idea what they were talking about.

As far as I was concerned, I had been away.
Now I was home.
Everything was as it should be.

Two days later, 9 September, marked the first anniversary of
my accident.

I'm sure my mum, Qelbes, Byron and others had previously
told me what had happened to me. Countless times.
But, for some reason, my brain decided that this was the day
that everything finally stuck.

I'd been hit by a car and almost died.
And I'd been fighting every day for a year to come home to
the man I loved.

At last I knew why the constant police presence outside
upset me.
Qelbes and Mum had to stop me from shouting at them.

Knowing now, what had been unknown for so long, I saw
myself a little differently.

My scars seemed more visible.
My wonky eye a little wonkier.
But I was no less determined to reclaim my life.

I felt stronger. Not weaker.

A rogue police car had tried to kill me.
And failed.
Nothing could stop me now.

24.

Being locked in a hotel room with your parents is a great idea for reality television.

To be fair, Mum and Qelbes were wonderful flatmates.
But those fifteen days felt like the longest month of my life.

Diversions were few.
I was unable to read books, or watch television.
My accident had left me with diplopia – double vision.
And my brain refused to let me concentrate – I couldn't follow what was happening.
Within a minute or two, the best movie ever made was reduced to light and noise.

My only reliable sources of entertainment were remote speech-therapy sessions, with my language pathologist in Brazil.

As prison sentences go, ours was short and pleasant.
But the claustrophobic sense of constrictive smallness, feeling trapped and powerless, was very real.

Romantic yearning building to anxiety, frustration and resentment.

Our luggage was recovered and returned, three days after we arrived.
Rather than gratefully slip into my own clothes, I refused to wear anything except the warm grey, complimentary Qatar Airways pyjamas.
A practical and comfortable choice for enforced home confinement.
However strange it may seem, my cosy fashion statement was also a personal protest at being denied access to fresh air.

Thankfully, we'd each received two pairs of pyjamas.
One for each international leg of our journey.
So, one pair could be washed while the other was being worn, theoretically.
And if I missed a laundry cycle, I finally had cause to be grateful that my traumatic brain injury had permanently robbed me of my sense of smell.

The monotony was galling.
Three meals of ennui per day.
The only break in our routine was being tested for Covid every now and then.

I assembled, disassembled and reassembled an infinite number of jigsaw puzzle pieces.

Byron sent me a miniature exercise bike machine, so I could continue my rehabilitation workouts.

Mum took a funny-saucy picture of me in the bath, holding
the bottle of champagne Byron had sent us.
I texted the photo to Byron.
Promised him we would wait to drink it together, inside our
Bondi apartment.

Two weeks passed.
We could almost taste freedom, when we received an
upsetting call from Australian health officials.
Despite all our Covid tests being negative, our quarantine
had been extended to twenty-five days.

Thank god for my mother.

She pounced on the phone and tongue-marched right up the
chain of command.
Demanding a medical explanation for this decision.
When none could be found, the authorities had no choice
but to release us on schedule.

I couldn't wait to show my parents the turquoise blue of the
Pacific Ocean, take them on a tour of my apartment.
Enjoy a walk along the beach.
Drink a real cup of coffee.
And kiss Byron.
Not in that order.

Our mandatory quarantine sentence officially ended at
11.59 pm on our fifteenth day.
Our bill was five thousand dollars.

Hotel management let us know we were welcome to stay till
the following morning, at no extra charge.
I made it clear that wouldn't be necessary.
My bags were already packed and sitting by the door.

After dinner I peeled off my grey prison pyjamas and threw
them in the bin.
I showered and, for the first time in forever, got dressed and
did my make-up.

Byron was waiting for us outside.

By midnight I was back in his arms.
Beneath the stars.

Byron drove me home.
It was just as I'd dreamed.
Everything seemed so exciting and new, yet so comforting
and familiar.

I thought my parents were going to stay in the guest room of
our apartment.
For some inexplicable reason they'd booked a hotel in
nearby Bondi Junction.
They'd taken a taxi, with all their baggage.

Maybe they wanted their own space.
Perfectly understandable.
I wanted Byron all to myself.

It was 1 am by the time we arrived at our apartment.
I couldn't describe the relief I felt, being back in my own
bed.

I was too tired to make love.
We both were.

I hadn't slept properly since the accident, let alone during
quarantine.
The past thirteen months had been mentally, emotionally
and physically stressful.
Trauma had soaked into my marrow.

But that night, pressed against Byron, unshackled my mind
and body.
Finally at peace.

My horrific ordeal was over.

I woke up refreshed. Rested.
So happy.

Being alive was delicious.
A cat yawning in sunshine.

I suffered just one mosquito pang of anxiety, when I realised Mum and Qelbes had taken my suitcase with them by mistake.

Then I found my dressing grown and remembered that it didn't matter.

I had everything I needed.

Our apartment was exactly as I'd left it.

Every piece of furniture, every single artwork was where I'd placed them.

My favourite clothes were hanging in my wardrobe, underwear folded in my dresser.

My shampoo and toothpaste had attained an unexpected vintage but otherwise my bathroom was identical to the day we departed on our European vacation, one year earlier.

I was home.

I was home.

I WAS HOME!

25.

I kept my promise.

Mum and Qelbes came over to our apartment to toast our
freedom with the fancy champagne Byron had gifted us
during quarantine.

It tasted like the breath of heaven.

I showed Mum around our apartment.
She didn't 'ooh' and 'aah' as much as I'd hoped, but she
loved it.
Then we took our overdue walk along the beach.

My parents could finally appreciate why I lived here.

When they were ready to leave, my mum said it would be
best if I went with them.
Back to the hotel.
I was confused.
But she insisted.
Something about my new routine.
New arrangements. Physiotherapy.
Something, something, something.

I didn't quite follow what she was saying.
Couldn't fathom why I wouldn't stay in my own home.
But I agreed to leave with them.

Byron bear-hugged me goodbye.
I revelled in how tall and broad he was.
His long arms wrapped and rewrapped me.

I loved it.

But later, in the taxi with my parents, I realised something odd.
Byron hadn't kissed me once since I got home.

Byron didn't kiss me the following week, either.

We had a great time, don't get me wrong.
My parents and I had a lovely time, and Byron was a big part of it.
Beautiful meals, great sightseeing, fun outings.
Ultimate Sydney-fest.

After two weeks in quarantine, Qelbes got to enjoy a real taste of Australia before he had to return to Brazil.
His business was keeping our family afloat, and he needed to get back to work.

Mum said she would stay on to help me adjust.
Whatever that meant.

Byron was kind and loving and generous, as always.
But … zero intimacy.
We didn't even hold hands.

Instead of going home each night, I stayed with my mum at her hotel.

My physiotherapist was located in the same building, so there were meaningful advantages to this.

But it still felt … wrong.

To have completed an epic return journey and be kept fifteen minutes apart from the man I loved.

Mum tiptoed around the matter.

Told me I needed to give Byron some space.

He'd been alone for so long.

He needed some time to adjust.

I didn't understand how this could be true, but I tried not to obsess about it.

Not easy.

After all the romantic cards, letters, gifts, messages and videos Byron had sent me, my expectations were understandably high.

Also, to be blunt, I hadn't spent a year away from my live-in boyfriend to revirginise myself.

I'd fought my way back from death's door to be with Byron.

And I had needs and desires.

26.

The following weekend was a big deal for me.
For us.

Byron threw a party to officially welcome me home.
Grace, Olivia, Margo, JP, Emma … all my Sydney friends
were there.
Each as bright and beautiful as I remembered.
More so.

It felt wonderful.
Beyond wonderful.
The happy ending to a Disney movie.

At first.

Heartfelt hugs.
Wave after wave of 'We missed you!'
'You're incredible!'

'You look amaaazing!'

Peppered with congratulatory platitudes.
A hailstorm of macarons.

I blinked and beamed.

My communication skills were a work in progress.
I fared better with reactive conversation.
Answering questions, rather than asking them.

So, I talked about myself, mostly.
Just repeated what I knew about my accident and recovery to
everybody who cared to listen.
A depressing record on a loop.

Laughter and murmurs behind me.
So many people talking at once.
I struggled to hear clearly.
With my impaired speech and Brazilian accent, people
struggled to understand me as well.
Friends who'd known me for years began to lean in, speaking
down to me like I was a child.
A clever toddler.

Grace sensed my anxiety and kept topping up my wine glass.
My tolerance to alcohol was still low.
After a few drinks I was even harder to understand.

Information processing slowed with every sip.
I laughed or didn't laugh at the wrong times.

Out of sync with the room.
I felt awkward.
Looked awkward.

Having recited the kind words of welcome and
congratulated me on how not dead I was, most friends
drifted away from me.

Chatting among themselves.
They seemed to have more fun when I wasn't in the mix.

If the party was a test, I'd failed.

I still loved seeing everybody.
It wasn't clear they felt the same way about me.
I was home yet still felt lost.

The combination of excitement, alcohol and social anxiety
had drained me completely.
Bone tired.
Brain tired.
Heart tired.

I slipped away. Into our bedroom.
Closed the door.
Got undressed.
Climbed into bed.

I woke up when Byron came into the room.
Our apartment was quiet at last.

He hesitated.

Then got into bed with me.

Being with Byron was all I needed to be happy.
I wanted him.
Needed him.

But he rejected me.

He wasn't ready, he said.
Still working through things, he said.

It was a very long night.

I returned to my mother's hotel room in the morning.
She read my face.

Frustrated, confused.

My homecoming party was both all I'd hoped and a stinging disappointment.
An epic New Year's Eve celebration that failed to live up to expectations.

I felt embarrassed. Hurt.
Yes, angry.

Robbed, cheated out of consummating our long-awaited reunion.
Denied the physical pleasure of making love.
The healing comfort and assurance of our sacred intimacy.

$\Diamond$

A busy week passed by.

Every day was a gruelling to-do list.
Medical appointments for my eyes, my broken limbs, my broken mind.
Physiotherapy.
Facial paralysis rehabilitation.
Personal training and Pilates.
Speech therapy.
Cognitive behavioural therapy.
Occupational therapy.
Sleep therapy.
Meeting with my social worker and, once a week, seeing my neuropsychologist.

An endless grimace of sweat and tears to be worthy of the memory of myself.
To recapture the happiness that once was mine.

My mum encouraged me, promised me everything would get better.

She and I had fun together.
Sometimes we had fun.
We tried to have fun.
We really tried.

We never wanted for anything.
Byron helped in any way he could.

He was kind.
But still didn't invite me home.
To our apartment.

His apartment.

◊

It was clear now that it was not our home. Just his.
Mum confirmed this for me.

I'd found it, we'd fallen in love with it together, and I'd made
it our home.
But he, not we, had paid for it.

Not all of this got through to me.
It made no sense for him to kick me out of our home after
being together for three years.
Being hit by a police car isn't grounds for divorce.

The romantic injustice was incomprehensible.
I could only repeat what was told to me without it really
sinking in.
Like talking to a bird.

It was our love nest that I missed.
Not the real estate.

Disinhibition. Impulsiveness. Immaturity. Insensitivity.
Just some of the acquired behaviours of a loving, intelligent
and accomplished human being whose brain has been
severely injured.
And is slowly trying to heal.

Unfiltered, 200-proof truth, according to Caroline.
No chaser.

Compulsive.
I started buying things I would never normally look twice at.
Expensive coats and handbags.
Two of each, thank you.

Mood swings.
Joy to anger to sadness, faster than a startled cat can find its
feet.

Self-focused.
All events seen through the lens of 'Yes, but is it good for
Caroline?'

Everything all at once.
Immediate wasn't fast enough.
I wanted to build Rome in the time it took to cook instant
noodles.

Conflicting emotions.
So easily upset.
Swollen with fear and desire.

My wounded psyche was a loveless marriage of self-belief and self-loathing.

But I wasn't a monster. I was just hurting.
Always hurting. Always feeling.
Confused by everything that had happened, was happening to me, that I couldn't control.

The explosive bloom of my first period while falling down an endless flight of stairs.

In some ways I was a teenager again.
Excited and earnest and innocent and generous and envious and insecure and overconfident and vulnerable and curious and secretive and honest and hopeful and overwhelmed.

I still loved me.

27.

I decided to take back what was mine.

I called Byron.
No, I sent him a text message.
He agreed to meet me at his apartment.
One week after my party.

I dressed to kill.
Make-up. Flawless.
Hair. *Chef's kiss*.
Perfume. Couldn't smell it but, sure. Check.

I don't know how I actually looked, limp-strutting to the
taxi in high heels.
But I felt like a movie star.
Jessica Rabbit had nothing on me.

My mission was straightforward.
Give Byron's heart a wake-up call.
Pick up where we left off.

> Step 1. Seduce my boyfriend.
> Step 2. He'd see what he was missing.
> Step 3. Restart our happily ever after.

Step 1 did not go well.

As soon as Byron saw me vamp through the door he was on
guard.
When I tried to press my case with my lips, he jerked his
face up and back.
As if to avoid being slapped.

He pushed my head away to his long arm's length
And held me there.

Byron said he was struggling emotionally with what had
happened.
He wasn't ready to go back to the way things were.
My accident had hurt him deeply.

Hurt him?

I wanted to laugh at this.
Wanted to scream at him.
And maybe I did.

But I also knew it was true.

Trauma wounds and stains in different ways.

Like grief, it doesn't always make sense how, where and when
it hits home.

Byron didn't spend an agonising year relearning how to eat, speak, walk.
He wasn't tied to a bed, wailing in agony.
It wasn't his skull split into two by a motorised meat cleaver.

But I know Byron witnessed much of this.
He faced the horror with his eyes open.

I'd slept through the worst of it.

Some men no longer see their wives sexually after childbirth.

I wondered how Byron saw me now.
Infantile, crippled, defective.
A burden?

Was I less attractive in person than my dating app profile photo now?

He said he still loved me.
But needed time.
Needed personal space.

I told him he also needed to find someone to talk to about this.
Professional help.
He promised he would.

28.

I was raised Catholic.
Limbo and purgatory are not vague concepts to me.

Purgatory is a place of pain and longing, on the periphery
of hell, where worthy but imperfect souls must be purified
before entering heaven.
Limbo is a nowhere place for unbaptised infants, tainted
with no sin of their own, yet damned to remain alone and
adrift between heaven and hell.

Figuratively speaking, both fates, I think, applied to me.

I tried to give Byron the space he needed to work through
whatever he was working through.
I still had faith in us.
In him.

Byron's love helped bring me back from the dead.
His love letters and videos had brought me home.
I trusted him to do what he needed to, so we could reclaim
our past and create a future together.

Byron didn't call.
No one called.

Until I repeatedly posted that I had survived a terrible accident, and I was really, really, really lonely.

Pathetic, perhaps.
But effective.

The upside of losing my inhibitions was that I no longer felt ashamed about speaking up about my needs.
It made no sense to suffer in silence.

Let's be honest, it never did.

Sydney friends were guilted into reaching out.
We caught up in groups at first, which was wonderful for me.
If I lost the flow of the table conversation I could sit back and enjoy everything as an audience member.

Just being present meant the world to me.

Some gatherings were better than others.
There were several friends who couldn't comprehend that, just because I was a tad slower to respond, and my speech was a little chaotic, I was not an imbecile.
I may not get the punchline of a joke at the same time as everyone else.
But I got it.
In the end.

Friends started talking over and around me, like I wasn't there.
They kept speaking down to me.
Even talking about me within earshot.

And when I tried to explain that I was neither a child nor a complete idiot, they were offended.

I wasn't as much fun as I used to be.
I could be a lot to deal with at times.

It hurt that my friends were bored by me.
Or felt awkward around me.
I just wanted to be near the people I cared about.
I wanted to feel cared about.

To be included.

I was trying my best.
Working hard, getting better every day.
But it wasn't fast enough.

Their affection became pity.
Pity became duty.
Duty became tiresome.

I was difficult.
A killjoy.
Word spread.

Covid-19 restrictions accelerated my social decline.
The group invitations dried up.

The brunches, lunches and cocktail parties still took place.
In private. In secret.
Without me.

Many of these same friends had donated generously to my
GoFundMe page.
But money was something they had plenty of.
Time and patience were far more precious.

They later claimed I chased them away with my strange
behaviour.
Maybe I did.
But the greater truth is that they gave up on me.

Within a short time only two friends would agree to see me.
Grace and Olivia.
One on one.

◇

The nuance and warmth of a face-to-face conversation
vanished.

My human interactions were confined to doctors, therapists
and personal trainers.
My two closest friends.
My semi-estranged boyfriend.
And my mum.

As far as I could tell, Earth's population had shrunk to less
than a dozen people.

◇

Then I got the call.

29.

Byron invited me out to dinner.
He wanted to take me somewhere special.

It was a date.
A real date.

My heart trilled with joy.

I chose the restaurant.
Just like I always did.
Alibi, in Woolloomooloo.

A beautiful vegan restaurant, inside a five-star hotel, on a heritage timber wharf that juts out into Sydney Harbour.

They had a dwarf Japanese maple tree laced with golden fairy lights.

I still had a thing for fairy lights.

Alibi was a special place for us.

Byron and I had attended the restaurant's grand opening two years earlier.
The owner hired a world-famous consulting chef from America.

He'd been flown out to help launch the restaurant.
But on opening night the American celebrity chef and his
stunning model girlfriend looked incredibly bored and
unhappy together.

They just scrolled through their phones.
Didn't talk.
Didn't look at each other.

The food was incredible and the ambience sublime.
We couldn't figure out why the guests of honour weren't
enjoying themselves.
It seemed both sad and comical.

Maybe they'd had an argument.

Were they breaking up?

◇

Byron was punctual.

He'd dressed beautifully. Very handsome.
Forgive me for stepping naked from the tepid bath of false
modesty, but we still looked amazing together.

Always the gentleman.
Byron opened the car door for me and helped me get seated.
Which was just as well.
My balance still wasn't great.
Falling into and out of buses had become an embarrassing
pastime.

Small talk in the car.
Compliments exchanged.
Excited.

The happiest I'd felt in a long time.

At the restaurant, Byron pulled out my chair for me.
We ordered pre-dinner cocktails.
Criminally delicious.

I wanted to clear the air about what had happened a week or
so earlier.
Not exactly an apology. An explanation.
I wanted to tell him how I felt.
Discuss how we could rebuild our relationship.

It wasn't complicated.
Not to me.
I still loved Byron. I wanted to be with him.

The accident had derailed both our lives.
But our plans had only been delayed, not cancelled.
I had defied, astounded the medical naysayers, and I was just
getting started.
I believed, I knew, in my healing bones, in the marrow of my
soul, that we could work through whatever difficulties lay
ahead.

We'd been happy together before the accident.
We could be happy again.

It was all so simple.
At least it was when I'd rehearsed it in my head.

The time came to put this into actual words.
I told Byron I had something I wanted to tell him.
My mind disagreed.

Nerves got the better of me.

I began to fidget.
Giggle.
Downcast eyes.

101

We'd ordered the tasting menu.

Every time I resolved to speak up another delicious morsel
would arrive.
The waiter would present each course as if selling us a rare
gem.
Then we'd try it.
Gush appropriately.
And repeat.

It was very hard to stay focused on what my heart needed
me to share.

Eventually Byron sensed my hesitation.

He asked me if I was okay.

Out it came.
All of it.
A burst pipe of emotion.

I could see by the way Byron looked at me that he still loved
me.
But not in the way I wanted to be loved.

Thankfully, he didn't string me along.
Pretend everything was fine. Would be fine.

He said that we were friends now.
Just friends.
Not lovers.

Not anymore.

As he spoke, his eyes understood my pain and longing.
How he was hurting me.

He started to cry.

That's when I realised that this special night together was
our break-up dinner.
Precious hope turned to sand inside my chest.

Byron had given up on me as well.

He told me that we'd had this difficult conversation before.
Several times.

Including when I'd tried to ravage him at his apartment, just a week earlier.

I had no memory of this.
But then, I had no memory of most things.

I would look at old photographs of the two of us and not remember what we'd been doing.
Where we were.
Why I'd been so happy.

Byron tried to explain that my accident had altered everything between us.
My accident had damaged him.
Changed him.
Though he couldn't say how.

He said we were both healing in our own way.
What we'd shared was now in the past.

I asked about all the love letters he had sent me.
The cards. The gifts.
The videos telling me he loved me and he was waiting for me.

That our home was waiting for me.
My whole life was waiting for me.

He'd made me believe in true love.
In our love.

Why did he say and write those things, so often, for so long?
Had he meant any of it?
Was everything he'd said to me a lie?

Byron confessed he was only trying to encourage me on my
recovery journey.
To motivate me to keep pushing, keep fighting, every day.
To make incremental improvements.
He didn't want me to give up on myself.

Compassion at its cruellest.

Heartbroken doesn't even begin to describe it.

I felt so alone.
Utterly lost.
Worthless.

I wished I'd died on that street in Barcelona.

Perhaps Byron sensed this because he promised he would
never abandon me.
He wanted us to remain close friends.
Not the gold medal I was promised. Had come so far to collect.
The participation ribbon.

I knew then that he didn't truly love me anymore.
Perhaps he did, once.
Perhaps.

But not now.

I kept asking him why.
But even if there was a why, Byron wasn't cold-hearted
enough to tell me to my face.

The new me, damaged me, wasn't attractive to him.
Old Me was perfect.
Byron wanted to marry and have four children with that
version of me.
But he didn't even want to kiss New Me.

The rest of our dinner date was comically hard.
We didn't really talk. Didn't look at each other.
Ruinous heartache.

Such wonderful food.
If anything, I ate too much.

Byron drove me back to the hotel in silence.
We both said 'goodnight'.
The word, only.

No hug.
No 'I love you'.
No goodbye kiss.

Byron didn't get out to open my door or help me to my feet.

◇

Every part of my being felt crushed.

My neck and shoulders surrendered to the pain.
Head drooped.
Bloated, off-balance.
I wanted to vomit.

Standing now, unsteadily.
Walking away slowly.
Careful not to trip and fall flat on my face.
Desperate to preserve any shred of dignity I had left.
Especially in front of a man who had changed my oversized
hospital nappies.

I had loved all of Byron with all of myself.
He was my forever.
Without him, without us, what was I?
All my romantic dreams were ashes and dust.

I kept it together. Barely.
Had to.
Just until I got back inside our hotel room.

Mum was waiting up for me.

I crawled straight into bed. Under the blankets.
Fully dressed.
Make-up on.

I tried to tell Mum.
Tried to tell her … 'Byron broke up with me.'
But I couldn't.
My throat closed over the first of the five words.
Kept trying.
Eyes red-wet.
Deep choking sobs shaking me by the shoulders, by the ribs.

Mum climbed into bed beside me and held me tight.
We ugly cried ourselves to sleep.

That night. That moment.
That was the first time that I truly felt broken.

> *Say you'll never let me go.*
> *Say you'll never let me go.*

30.

Byron ripped my heart open and spat in it.

Then, to show there were no hard feelings, he set up a
WhatsApp group for friends to support my recovery with
encouraging messages.

He helped to edit and post a video montage.
Pre-accident. The aftermath.
Hospital stays.
And rehabilitation.
It was set to 'Angel By The Wings' by Sia.

Such a beautiful song.
Apparently Sia wrote it for a documentary about a young
Kazakh girl who defied the patriarchy by training a golden
eagle to hunt foxes.

Was I the girl, the eagle or the fox?

Byron's friends loved it.

> **What an incredible recovery**
> **Caroline and such amazing**
> **support from Byron!**
>
> **Your grit and determination is**
> **absolutely incredible Caroline ...**
> **You honestly are an inspiration ...**

Byron, you too are just
amazing ...

Absolutely incredible! Caroline we
are so pleased with your recovery,
inspired by your strength and
determination ...
Byron, so proud of you ...

Caroline you are an incredibly
strong human! ... Byron, you too
are an inspiration my friend!

Bitter and hurt, I broke my silence.

I posted on the WhatsApp group that Byron had broken up
with me.
We were no longer together.
Even though I'd believed we'd always be together.
That we'd get married.

Why had he waited till I'd come home to him?
Travelled halfway around the world during a pandemic.
To tell me there was no place for me in his heart.
Or in the home we'd made together.

I acknowledged Byron's generosity.
I was genuinely grateful for his ongoing help.

But then I made a dark joke – a clumsy, childish double entendre.
That it was so typical for men to lose interest in a woman after an accident.

I don't know if my heartbreak had stirred up the rage I felt about the way Lars had treated my mother.
Or if I was thinking about something else.

Byron was angry with me. Embarrassed.
I had violated group messaging protocol, he said.
This group chat was about me, not for me.

His friends publicly criticised me.
Chastised, patronised me.
Mansplaining the tragedy to the victim in order to defend Byron.

Was I aware that Byron had witnessed my accident and stood vigil beside my mother for a few months?

Did I know that Byron had lost the love of his life in a terrible car accident and needed to move on?

In their eyes, Byron was a saint.
Deserving of my eternal gratitude and everyone's sympathy.

But me?

I was damaged goods, shopsoiled and stupid.
And they were no longer bound to me by Byron's affection.

In their eyes, my heartbreak, like my physical and mental disabilities, was an acceptable casualty.

I was disposable.
A nuisance.
A ghost to be exorcised.

◇

Not one of Byron's male friends expressed any sorrow for the break-up.
They didn't seem remotely surprised that I'd been tossed aside so soon after my homecoming party.

No one reached out to ask if I was okay.

Every public response contained a tacit endorsement of Byron's decision to break up with me.
To them, it was inevitable.

So, they either knew it was over between Byron and me well before I did.
Or they just didn't care.
Perhaps both.

They wanted their friend back.
They wanted his ex-girlfriend gone.

One by one, they left my WhatsApp recovery support group chat.
Men. Women.
All of them.

◇

Margo told everyone it was time to move on.
High time.

I heard she'd set up a new private WhatsApp group, also
called 'Besties'.
Invited everyone but me.

Byron's friends may not have liked me very much right then,
but they knew a cheap shot when they saw one.
Grace would have nothing to do with it.
Only two or three girls joined.
Byron spoke to one of them about the cruelty of this gesture.
The new group was soon deleted.

31.

Grace took me out to dinner to cheer me up.
We went to Yulli's, an amazing vegan bar and restaurant in
Surry Hills.
I loved it.

She kept telling me not to think about Byron anymore.
He and I were just 'good friends' now.
I should focus on my recovery.
That's all that mattered.

Grace suggested I get another tattoo.
Cover up the large scar on my left shoulder.
She'd mentioned this more than once.

I liked tattoos. Already had several.
But her saying this, again and again, made me feel self-
conscious about my scars.
All my scars.
Visible and invisible.

Just then, Taika Waititi walked in.
My peanut-butter-coated brain was still trying to put a name
to his world-famous face, when Grace hauled me out of my
seat for a selfie.
Taika, very kindly, gave us the time of day.

While we were eating, I heard Grace gasp.
She whisper-shouted that Taika was dining with Natalie
Portman.
The Natalie Portman!

They were seated in the darkest, farthest corner of the
restaurant.
I couldn't make out anyone. Anything.

Grace knew how much I adored Natalie.
She encouraged me to walk over and say hello.
But I wouldn't.

I couldn't.

Even if I didn't trip and knock over tables and chairs on my
way back there.
A huge assumption in itself.
My speaking ability was still painfully limited.
Especially under pressure.

I was horrified at the thought of meeting one of my heroes
and then gushing unintelligible gibberish.
Squawking and gagging at her.
A parrot choking on a walnut.

After everyone had turned their back on me.
The thought of creeping out the woman I'd looked up to for
so long.
I couldn't bear it.

Almost-but-not-quite meeting Natalie was still exciting.
I tagged her in our selfie with Taika, even though she wasn't
in it.
Another violation of social media protocol.

At one level, I was a starstruck teenager again.
But, somewhere, deep inside, this encounter started wheels
turning.

I didn't remember No Saints.
At all.
But I sensed that there was something that I needed to look
into, needed to do.
Something important.

As soon as I got home, I powered up my old laptop.
Determined to search my old files.
Emails. Messages.
Everything.

I didn't know what I was looking for, or what I'd find.

But until recently I believed I existed to love Byron and be
loved by him.
If that wasn't true, then I had nothing but questions.

I opened my laptop.
Fingertips poised above the keyboard.

Dark screen.
Locked out.

Couldn't remember the damn password.

32.

I don't know how deeply you have to love someone to hate them as much as I hated Byron after he broke up with me.

And yet.
Just couldn't shake my attachment to him.
Couldn't give up on the dreams we'd shared.
Dreams I'd thought we'd shared.

Byron continued to be a gentleman.
He let my mum know he was available to help us with whatever.
Whenever.

My domestic situation was untenable.
I'd planned on being back in our Bondi apartment.
Mum was supposed to be staying in the guest room.
Cosy as a cat on a cushion.

Instead, Mum and I were still sharing a hotel room that felt smaller by the day.
Even as a stopgap it was costing a fortune.

What we needed most, what I needed, was somewhere to live.
A place of my own.

Mum and I began the apartment treasure hunt.

I still wanted to stay in Bondi.
That was my dream, even before I met Byron.

My brand-new ex-boyfriend shocked us both by saying he would prefer me to live nearby.
In case I needed help.

I felt conflicted.
On the one hand, I had never loved anyone as much as I'd loved Byron.
Plus, other than Grace and Olivia, he was all I had.

But, on the other hand, I wanted him to be eaten alive by bullet ants.

Apartment hunting wasn't made any easier by my limited mobility.
Stairs were my enemy.

We saw a few listings. Nothing felt right.

Byron suggested a place he thought was suitable.
It was close by and affordable.
But also, kind of meh.
Full of trip hazards.

I stumbled several times during the open house.
Mum got very upset.
Byron looked sheepish.

I found a very nice apartment.
Fabulous location.
Two large, well-lit bedrooms.
Fully furnished.

A little more expensive.
But I loved it.

Under six minutes to the beach.
Less than ten from Byron's home.

It felt weird saying 'Byron's home'.

I secured the apartment, but there were some timing issues.
My planned move-in date and our hotel booking did not align.
We were in a tight spot.

Byron offered to help us out.

In a strange twist, Mum and I stayed at Byron's apartment.
We shared the bed in the guest room.
For six days and nights.

Byron did everything to make us feel at home.
But it was already my home, so ... you know.
Surreal.

It was not a very merry Christmas.

I wasn't invited to celebrate with Byron's family this year.
Obviously.

Mum decorated a Christmas tree at my new apartment to
make it seem a little festive.

On the day before Christmas, I had lunch with Grace and
Olivia at the local pub.
Then they dropped by my new place to exchange presents
and hugs.

It meant a lot to me, and to my mum.

I gave each of my besties a pair of adorable pyjamas.
I'd become something of a pyjama expert.
Ask anyone.

Mum accepted Byron's surprise invitation to take us
Christmas shopping.
And for us to have dinner with him at his apartment on
Christmas Eve.
My heart felt a little seasick.

Thankfully, Byron and I didn't cook Christmas dinner
together.
He ordered in.

Delicious.

Just the three of us.
Strange, but not unpleasant.
We talked, we laughed.
Truth be told, it was kind of lovely.

Byron gave me some earrings.
Plus the coffee maker I'd wanted for the housewarming party
I never had.
He knew how I liked to start my day.

Mum gave me a pair of sunglasses.

Identical to the sunglasses that had been pulverised to
crumbs and glitter when the police car hit me.

I gave Mum a white linen dress that she'd chosen.
Perfect for breezy walks along the beach.

Mum and I gave Byron some shorts.
He has nice legs.

On Christmas Day, Mum and I enjoyed a second Christmas
dinner together at a local restaurant.

It wasn't much, as festive celebrations go.
But it was nice.

We were thankful for each other.

I'd spent my three previous New Year's Eves with Byron.
Two epic parties.
One in South Africa.
One in Brazil.
Though I'd slept through our last New Year's Eve, in Spain.

This year, Byron was heading up the coast to the Northern Rivers.
With all his friends. My former friends.
They were ringing in the New Year in style.

It was madness on my part, but I so badly wanted to go with him.

I was certain someone would invite Mum and me to a party in Sydney.
Perhaps dinner.
Drinks and nibbles. Something. Anything.
But, no.

We were on our own.

Mum was in bed by nine.
I stayed up, spooning a sofa cushion.
Watching Sydney's famous midnight fireworks on television.
It was a little sad.
No, very sad.

Easily the third worst New Year's Eve I'd ever experienced.
After the time I'd spent the night stuck on a boat with no bathroom.

And of course, the previous year, when I was in a coma.
Wearing a soiled adult nappy.

New Year's Day was overcast.
The beach was strangely empty.

Mum encouraged me to swim in the sea.
Let the waves wash away a bad year.
Start fresh.

It felt good.

33.

Our original repatriation plan, as I understood it:
Mum would escort me home safely to Byron.
She'd stay with us for a couple of weeks, enjoying Australian
hospitality while I settled into my new rehab routine.
Then she'd fly back to Brazil, sun-kissed and serene.

Mum spent almost four months in a hotel.
Another two months in my new apartment.

All this, on top of the year grafted to my bedside.
In Barcelona.
Curitiba.
Caxias do Sul.

She'd put her entire life on hold for me.

My day-to-day was so much smaller now, but it was all I
could handle.
And handle it, I did.
Standing on my own feet again.
Proving I could look after myself.

I let Mum know I felt it was time to restart my adulthood.
I wanted to be an independent single woman again.

My mother knew this day would come.
Hoped and prayed it would come.
And dreaded it.

We talked through every emergency scenario.
She triple-checked that I knew what I was doing.
That I had everything I could possibly need.
Then she flew home to Brazil.

Looking back at me the entire flight.

After almost eighteen months of being bandaged and fussed over, I enjoyed the feeling of flying solo.

But I still missed my mum.

Terribly.

34.

When my life was perfect, the world seemed perfect.
When I was broken, I saw the world as it is.

I moved slower now.
Slow enough to notice things.

Bondi felt different, looked different.

Still picturesque, still vibrant.
But not quite as friendly.
Not quite as clean.
Not as safe.

The cosmetic veneer had slipped.
Cracks, visible now in daylight.
And in the shadows.

I could see the scar tissue connecting rich and poor,
glamorous and ordinary.

The beautiful people who once defined this dynamic city
beach for me, whom I wanted to emulate, now seemed
incredibly shallow.

Hollow.
In a hurry, going nowhere.

I was never blind to the people who made everything work.
But now they were the only ones who saw me.
Shopkeepers, streetsweepers, council workers.
Good people doing hard, thankless work with a smile.
I loved them for that.

When you have so few friends, every smile matters.
Every helping hand is an act of grace.

My dwindling social life migrated to social media.
To no one's surprise, my fractured mind didn't thrive
online either.

My posts were often garbled.
Overly self-focused.
An off-putting blend of grandiosity and nit-pickery.

Repetitive.
So repetitive.

I couldn't comprehend the subtle politics of friendship.
Struggled to read the room.
Thin-skinned, hotblooded.
I would take so many things the wrong way.
Get upset. ALL CAPS.

And I was frequently guilty of the greatest of all sins.
Telling people the unfiltered truth.

Virtual or otherwise, damaged me wasn't the best company.
I got it.

But I was trying.
I really was.

35.

Haters never sleep.
The anonymous messages kept coming.

> Beautiful Caroline ... Your
> friends Byron and Olivia are
> sleeping together, both when
> you were in Brazil and also since
> you're living in Australia. Byron
> also had another girlfriend, Carla,
> for several months last year. He
> told everyone in January that
> you broke up, so we thought him
> being with other women was
> OK, but now I see your posts and
> pictures of allllll his messages
> saying, 'I love you', I don't believe
> him anymore ☹☹☹

My mother got them as well.
In both English and Portuguese.

> All of Byron's friends think it was
> the biggest mistake for Caroline
> to come back to Australia.

◊

Thank god for Grace.

She dropped by to see if I was okay.

I asked her about the hateful messages I'd received.

Were Olivia and Byron really together while I was in hospital? Were they together now?

Grace thought it was probably true, might be true.

She didn't know for sure.

No. I couldn't bring myself to believe it.

Olivia wouldn't do that to me.

I was determined not to let troll gossip ruin my birthday.

It was the one thing I had to look forward to.

I wanted to make a big splash.

After the mass friendship exodus following my welcome home party, and my break-up with Byron, I wanted everyone to know I was still alive.

That I was improving daily.

I was worthy of their friendship.

That I could be fun again.

I decided to host a dinner party at Eden, an open-air vegan restaurant near me with plenty of wow-factor.

I invited everyone I knew and told them to invite everyone they knew.

And I do mean everyone.

Former colleagues.

Former flatmates.
Byron, and all the friends I'd shared with Byron.
Including Margo.

Even the men who had openly criticised me on my recovery
group chat.
I wanted to give everybody a second chance to be my friend.

I wanted everybody to give me a second chance.

By now, everyone knew that Byron and I had broken up.
And it was an open secret that Byron had been seeing
someone else while I was in hospital.
Friends and family had seen the nasty comments I'd received
online.

It didn't sit well with my two loyal girlfriends.

Grace and Olivia let me know they wouldn't attend the party
if Byron's friends were going to be there.
We made plans to celebrate on our own.

Fourteen people accepted my invitation.
Not a huge RSVP percentage, but I was thrilled.

A Brazilian friend of my aunt's worked at Zimmermann.
She helped me find a gorgeous dress at 50 per cent discount.

My dinner party was really coming together.

Then, a few days before my birthday, it started to rain.
It didn't stop.

An ocean fell out of the sky.
Roads and bridges were cut off.
Houses were flooding.
For someone like me, with limited mobility, dependent on
outside help, it was frightening.

The manager at Eden got in touch.
She apologised, but said they had to close their open-air
dining area.
In just forty-eight hours it had turned into a pool with a
swim-up bar.
However, she promised me they would keep their kitchen
open.
They'd deliver food to my home, in the pouring rain if need
be.
Did I want to go ahead with my birthday dinner plans?

You bet I did.
Deluge be damned.

I wasn't sure if anyone would show up after I changed the
dinner venue to my modest apartment.

Thirteen guests braved the wild weather.
God knows where they parked.

The stormwater drains were overflowing.
White-water rafting was now possible down most Bondi streets.

Maybe it wasn't the party to end all parties.
But it meant the world to me.
The guests were fun.
The food was incredible.
And that killer dress.

So grateful.

The next day was my actual birthday.
I returned to Yulli's for my girls' birthday lunch with Grace and Olivia.
It was wonderful, even without Taika Waititi and Natalie Portman.

Except Olivia didn't show.

36.

After my birthday dinner party triumph I was hopeful I'd
resume a more normal social life.
Too hopeful.

Still no regular social contact with anyone, apart from Grace
and Byron.

I'm not even sure if you'd describe my interactions with
Byron as social.
More of a love/hate/like/dislike/beholden/resented guardian
angel dynamic.

Olivia was increasingly hard to pin down.
We'd text every now and then, but we never seemed to be in
the same place at the same time.
Out of respect for our friendship I never brought up the
rumours that she and Byron had hooked up.
I wanted to give her the benefit of the doubt.
But the fact that she was avoiding me …

Most old friends and colleagues simply cut me off.
Others used the Covid lockdown defence to keep me at bay.
But, for many, it was no one's fault.
Just life and work and distance.
Everyone had their own plans, their own problems.

I'd been away for a year.
People had relocated, changed jobs, got married.
Started families.
Moved on.

Without me.

Laura, my Kiwi work-bestie, returned to New Zealand while
I was in Brazil.
At the time I didn't know how to reconnect.
I really could have used a friend like her.

I was lonely.
Needed companionship.
Someone to cuddle up with after a painful day of
physiotherapy.

I wanted to adopt a cat.

When I told Byron he treated me like a child.
Said I wasn't ready to have a pet.
I could barely look after myself, let alone another lifeform.
He semi-politely reminded me that I couldn't even boil water
safely.
I'd already set fire to a childproof crockpot.
For this reason, safely pre-prepared meals were now
delivered to me by the NDIS, the National Disability
Insurance Scheme.
Byron was pretty sure the NDIS wouldn't deliver cat food.

'You definitely shouldn't adopt a cat,' he insisted.

I did it anyway.
Best decision ever.

Sundy was just what I needed.
And I like to think I was just what she needed as well.

A dark ginger and black tabby.
Sundy was gentle and loving.
The most creative and spontaneous sleeper I've ever seen.
She could nap anywhere, any time.
Stretched out, around and over any warm surface with
Dali-esque languor.
Squished into the bottom of any container like a dropped
cake.

I was so happy to have an affectionate friend who never
judged or criticised me.
The all-seeing internet trolls, not so much.
And they let my mum know.

> **Hi there. Maybe you could think
> about actually supporting your
> disabled daughter, like a proper
> mother, instead of dumping
> her in Australia to live with no
> friends and just a dirty street cat
> for company.**

THE FLATMATE

By the following winter, Australia's increasingly severe Covid lockdown protocols had left me extremely isolated.

Mum agreed with Byron's suggestion that I should get a flatmate.
Byron and Grace offered to help me find someone who, in exchange for reduced rent, would be willing to be a live-in companion of sorts.

A friendly face.
Someone to talk to.
Offer me a little help, from time to time.

Grace found the perfect flatmate.
A girl named Paloma.
She was a few years younger than me.
Smart, energetic.
Worked from home.

Also, Brazilian. And bilingual.
Which helped a lot.

Sundy loved her as well.

Since my accident I had boundary issues.

Overjoyed to have someone to hang out with, I was guilty of treating Paloma as a mail-order best friend.

At first, it was wonderful.

Paloma and I would have coffee together.
We would go to the gym together.
Sometimes we'd eat dinner and watch TV with Sundy.

Lockdown pushed many flatmates and even marriages to the brink.
But ours got there faster.

In addition to being clingy, I had the emotional maturity of an eight-year-old.
I also suffered from mood swings.
Horrible for me, and for those around me.
But quite normal for someone with a traumatic brain injury.
Especially during the first few years of recovery.

Like most people with brain injuries, depression, pain and insomnia were constant battles for me.

I was taking a prescribed antidepressant medication called venlafaxine, to ease my nerve pain, elevate my mood and help me sleep.

A negative side effect of venlafaxine that I experienced was that I was more prone to emotional outbursts.

I could become angry when I was upset or felt confused or threatened.

During these outbursts I couldn't be trusted to make safe choices.
Couldn't trust myself.
This worried my mum no end.

Byron had agreed to become my financial guardian, using his professional knowledge to supervise my spending and saving habits.
He made sure I paid my bills and taxes, stuck to a reasonable budget, and didn't drain my entire bank account on a whim.

Grace helped me set up a second personal bank account
for minor expenses to save me the indignity of running to
Byron when I wanted a cup of coffee and a chocolate muffin.

Having your ex control your money is a horrible and intractable entanglement.
Not a recipe for peace and harmony.
Whenever Byron refused to give me the money I asked for.
Or didn't release the funds fast enough.
I would initiate an intense one-sided argument.

A simple misunderstanding could run from chill to inferno in a heartbeat.

Before Paloma agreed to move in, Byron explained to her that disagreements with me could get heated.

He made her promise to call him if I became upset. About anything.
He also told her how to help calm things down before they escalated.

But volcanic foreknowledge doesn't make an eruption any less jarring.

I'd always done my remote speech therapy sessions in the living room.

Paloma asked me to move these online appointments into my bedroom.
She didn't enjoy listening to my weird noises and loud verbal exercises.

I understood where she was coming from.
Still a little miffed.
I'd never felt embarrassed about my speech therapy exercises.
Until then.

Paloma also didn't like my support worker hanging around.
She felt her personal space was being violated.

I didn't know how to respond to this.
I needed the help.
My support worker was essential for my wellbeing.

Paloma was getting under my skin as well.

She started inviting friends over to our apartment.
That didn't bother me at all. I was delighted.
The more people the better.
Also, Paloma's friends were wonderful – we all clicked.
So I thought.

Not sure what I did or said, but Paloma made a point of not including me in these social gatherings.

Pretty awkward, really, as I was usually less than three metres away.
Even my cat had been invited.

Paloma began sulking whenever I entered her field of vision.
Slipping back into her bedroom like a shy octopus.
She was never available to chat anymore, let alone help me with anything.

It didn't feel like she was holding up her end of our deal.

When Paloma's boyfriend stayed over on Friday nights, they had a thing for morning sex.
I was jealous. I admit it.
Byron's rejection was just the beginning.
I'd been put on the shelf, an honorary nun, thanks to the chastity belt of sexual ableism.

But honestly, who wants to wake up to loud moaning every Saturday?

One night, Byron came over to watch a movie with us.
I was sitting between Byron and Paloma.
Everyone was getting along famously.

At some point, Byron and Paloma started chatting casually
to each other.
Just friendly back and forth.
It was still difficult for me to watch television without 100
per cent concentration.
I was trying very hard to follow what was happening in the
movie, and their banter was throwing me off.
Instead of simply asking them to be quiet, or continue their
conversation in another room, I lost my temper.
I screamed at them to shut up.

Byron smoothed things over, but it was never the same after
that.

Paloma was pleasant enough.

But she stayed in her room almost all the time.
She changed her gym schedule so we wouldn't see each other
there, either.

Sensing that our relationship was in jeopardy, I tried to
mend fences with her.
Politely ambushing her when she popped into the kitchen to
make herself a coffee.

I asked her if everything was okay between us.
Was she still happy living with me?

Paloma assured me that everything was peachy.
While we were chatting, she used her smartphone to send
me the money for the next two weeks' rent.
I was relieved.

Maybe we weren't the best flatmates in the world.
But I liked having Paloma around.
I wanted things to get back to the way they'd been at the
outset.

Three hours later, Paloma texted me to let me know she'd
found another apartment.
She was moving out in two days.
She wanted the money she'd just paid me returned
immediately.
Plus, her two weeks' bond.

I was stunned.

I'd been lied to.
Betrayed again.

When I got home that afternoon, I knocked on Paloma's door.
I just wanted to ask her what was going on, clear the air.

I needed to understand what had suddenly changed her
mind.
Still hoped we could talk it all out.

But Paloma didn't want to talk to me.
When I begged, then insisted, she slammed her door in my
face.

I stopped the door from hitting me with my hands and forearms.

Talking became shouting.

She wouldn't tell me what happened and started screaming at me to go away.
Go where?
I was in my own home.

She started videoing me with her phone.
I could feel my face turning red, my throat swelling.
Everything was going black, I started to shake.
Couldn't move my feet.
I knew I was shouting, but didn't know what I was saying, or whether I was speaking English or Portuguese.
Even using words at all.

Every cell in my mind and body was overwhelmed and trembling.
An orgasm of dark rage.

It didn't stop until Paloma shoved me backwards and I fell heavily onto the floor.
My glasses, once again, flying off my head.

Paloma locked herself inside her bedroom and called the police and Byron.
In that order.

Byron arrived on the scene to act as peace broker.
But he was too late.
The damage was done.

The police officers watched Paloma's video.
I have to assume she'd deleted the part where she pushed me
to the ground.

I still wasn't able to speak.
The police officers accepted Byron's explanation that my
traumatic brain injury was behind my emotional verbal tirade.

Nevertheless, my behaviour was deemed a danger to Paloma.
I was served with a temporary restraining order.
Forbidding me from approaching Paloma or speaking to her.
I had to leave my home and stay away while she arranged for
her belongings to be collected.

Sundy and I hid out at Byron's apartment like fugitives.

I felt ashamed, angry.
Powerless.

I knew I was at fault.
My meltdown was inexcusable, unacceptable.
But the fact that I had no way of controlling my feelings was
humiliating and terrifying.

And the belief that I couldn't trust anybody anymore was
soul destroying.

All I wanted was to make new friends.
All I did was push people away.

I began to wonder if I could maintain any kind of
meaningful friendship.
If I could even hope to find love.
Ever again.

37.

I couldn't stand my life anymore.
It shocked me to admit it, but I hated Bondi now.

I needed to go somewhere.
Anywhere.
Otherwise, I was going to explode.

Byron declared I wasn't capable of travelling by myself.
It wasn't safe, he said.

He pointed out that I frequently fell over in the street, and
while getting on and off buses, and stepping out of taxis, and
using stairs of any kind.
That I had trouble remembering directions.
I wasn't good under pressure.
My communication skills were poor.
That I'd been scammed by online con artists more than
once.

Byron was telling the truth.
The miserable truth.
I knew he was genuinely concerned.
Harping on the negative was his way of expressing love.

But I was sick of being told what I was and what I wasn't.
What I could and couldn't do.

People kept telling me how well I was doing.
How proud I should be.
What an inspiration I was to them.

But the grim reality was that I had lost everything.
I was living alone.
Ate all my meals alone.
On a two-bedroom desert island.

The man I'd hoped to marry had dumped me.
I had little to no chance of meeting anyone new.
Virtually no friends.
No job.
No prospects.

I struggled with the most basic tasks.
Couldn't use the oven or stove.
Finally had my driver's licence back. But now I couldn't drive.
Could barely push a supermarket trolley without mass casualties.

Just getting through an ordinary day required monumental effort and a great deal of outside help.

Opening a can of cat food felt like a genuine achievement.

When I ran into former friends, they would wish me well.
But they were really wishing me away from them.

And even my closest friends, I suspect, were wishing something far more specific and insidious.

They wanted me to recover fully, as soon as possible.
Or not recover at all.

If my brain injury fully healed, I would be fine.
Everything would be normal once more.
They could all relax and enjoy Old Caroline again.
She was clever and sexy and fun.

If my brain injury remained severe and did not improve, then I would not be aware of my limitations.
This would lower my levels of frustration and make New Caroline easier to manage.

There was a danger zone everyone wanted me to avoid, for my sake.
And theirs.
Almost but not quite fully recovering from my brain injury.
Where you know, with bitter clarity, who you were and everything that's wrong with you now.

So many people trapped in this abyss of cruel awareness and utter helplessness are unable to cope with the agonising frustration and humiliation of their brain injury.
Unable to accept their reduced capacity for thought and action.
They obsess on the fractured landscape of their own mind.
The likelihood of ending their suffering by unnatural means jumps by 400 per cent.

In the United States, where guns are bought and sold like sandwiches, the most common cause of death for people with traumatic brain injuries like mine is suicide by firearm. Just like dear Rosana.

I booked a flight to America.

Don't worry, I wasn't going to kill myself.
Although god knows I'd often wished I was dead.

But I didn't crave death.
I craved joy and human connection.

New reasons to live.

I finally made it to Orlando.
Realised my childhood wish.
Went to Walt Disney World.

Mum met up with me and we had a wonderful time.
I wore the mouse ears and everything.

I'd been dreaming of this day since I was seven.
I couldn't remember Mickey, Minnie, Donald and Goofy's names.
But my inner child recognised them immediately.
They made me smile.

An alternate cartoon reality that finally delivered the freedom to be happy.

Everybody was acting just like me for a change.
No one looked down on me or judged my appearance.
We were all there to have fun.

A friendly stranger asked me to take a picture of him and his girlfriend.
Then he surprised us both by proposing.
I kind of screwed up the video in all the excitement.
But it was sweet and lovely.

The first time someone had asked me for help since my accident.

There's a lot to be said for embracing your innate sense of joy and wonder.
And having faith in other people to do the same.

I wished real life, adult life, was all about having fun together.
Less about having more, doing more, being more.
Being perfect.

38.

I kept travelling.
It wasn't easy.
There were some close calls.
I fell over. More than once.
Got lost. Got ripped off.
Some days were hard.

But stopping was harder.

Brazil, United Kingdom, Switzerland, Qatar, Portugal.
I didn't know what I was looking for.
Until I arrived in Spain.

I decided to complete the journey I'd started with Byron.

I landed in Ibiza.
Went to the shows.
It wasn't what I'd imagined.
For the first time in years, the music didn't pull me in.

Anne Elliot standing at the back of the dance party.

I returned to Barcelona.
Walked the streets like a ghost.

None of it made sense.
Nothing felt like I thought it would.
Hoped it would.

There was no closure.

I found myself on the Via Laietana.
At the pedestrian crossing where a speeding police car had
destroyed my life.

I felt no connection to this place.
And yet, there I stood.
Unable to cross the street.

A police car pulled up a few metres away.
Two officers got out quickly and walked over.
But they weren't there for me.

They approached a man in his thirties and started
questioning him.
I couldn't understand what was going on.
But I needed to leave.

I had a taxi driver follow my phantom ambulance to the
hospital.
Where I'd spent so many months in pain and darkness.
It was just yesterday.
It was forever ago.

The hospital seemed big and small at the same time.
Nothing looked familiar.
I met with Dr Gerardo Conesa Bertrán.
The famous neurosurgeon who'd saved my life.
He was kind and brilliant.
And wonderful.

Dr Bertrán had movie star hair.
I'm surprised my mum never mentioned this.

I reunited with Maribel, Christina, Maria and Bárbaro.
The four incredible nurses who had cared for me, night and day.

Their buoyant hearts had kept my mother's spirits afloat.

I didn't recognise any of them.
But that didn't bother them one bit.
They welcomed me like a prodigal daughter.
Hugging, smiling, laughing.
Kissing, kissing, kissing my cheek.

For once, I wasn't a disappointment to old friends.

Just by being alive.
By finding my way back to them.
I had exceeded all expectations.

They gave me the most precious gift.
Letting me see myself through their eyes.

I was a living miracle.
The embodiment of hope.
Of victory against overwhelming odds.
I was the reason they got up every morning to do their impossible job.

It was beautiful.
I was beautiful.

I wished I could make my mum feel the way I felt in that moment.

When I got back to Bondi, I had a mission.

39.

BRAIN-DAMAGED DETECTIVE

A confusing jumble of passwords saved on my phone.

I opened my laptop and tried every single one.

It took a long time.

A very long time.

My computer password turned out to be a misspelling of the word 'proficiency'.
How apt.

What to do with this illuminated screen ...
Where to begin?

I opened my browser.
The last searches I'd made before my accident popped up.
Eight separate web pages on the exact same subject.

How to have an orgasm during sex.

Not at all what I'd expected to find.
I called Byron.
Asked him if I'd ever had an orgasm during sex.

He said yes.
At least once.
He was almost certain.

For the very first time, I started to question our relationship.
Our narrative suddenly didn't seem quite as perfect.

I read all eight web articles.
Then I bought a vibrator.

Smart move.

My laptop was a gold sluice of information.
Plucking precious details from gigabytes of pay dirt.

I'd made detailed notes on everything.
Taken photos of everyone.
Going back to pre-forever.

I found out that I'd changed my mind about becoming a civil
engineer.
Switched to a business degree in administration,
management and operations.
Still building big things with maths, but not out of concrete
and steel.

I'd also been to Australia before.

When I was changing degrees.

I saved up so I could take a break.

That's when I'd spoken to my friend, Marcos.

That's when I worked for the advertising company, where I was robbed by junkies on the Friday before the Day of the Dead.

Looking back, it was clear I didn't have the best time during my first visit.

To fulfil the study component of my student visa I completed the Cambridge English course.

I thought I'd completed this exam in Brazil, but it happened later, in Manly. I felt it was kind of a joke.

A waste of time and money I didn't have.

Honestly, my *Friends* language school was superior in every way.

Everything was so expensive in Australia compared to Brazil.

To earn enough to stay in Sydney I worked long shifts as a waitress in a grotty little restaurant.

Had a sleazy boss.

Survived on cheap junk food.

Put on tonnes of weight.

My skin broke out.

And yet, wrongness be damned, I loved it.

So, so much.

I belonged here.
Before boarding my flight home I'd made a plan to come back.

Sooner the better.

◇

In Porto Alegre I worked harder than ever.
Full-time job while studying full time at uni.

My head hummed like a beehive.

No graduation vacation for me, thank you.
My sole objective was to move to Australia.

Joined a real estate firm.
I'd been told it was the fastest way to make money without a gun.

Rookie agent.
Headful of numbers.
Hustling like a veteran.
Seven days and nights a week.

Determined to reach my impossible goal, within a year.

Black pants, white blouse.
High heel sandals.
No lipstick. No nonsense.
Always be closing.

I didn't expect to fall in love.

◇

Joaquim. That was his name.

He was beautiful. Literally beautiful.
A male model.
And no one makes models like we do in Brazil.

Joaquim was also a super-nerd.
Very sweet. And ambitious.
A software engineer who'd already started his own company.

No time for romance.
Zero.
But we couldn't stay away from each other.

I was completely upfront about my plans.
Even while catching my breath between kisses.
I would be on a plane to Sydney in five months.

Nothing, and no one, was going to stop me.

Hard work pays off.

When my visa deadline arrived, I'd closed almost six million dollars in sales.
A top five agent for our national company.
Better numbers than realtors twice my age.
My boss begged me to stay.

But even though it was always about the money.
It was never about the money.

I was going to Australia.

Joaquim wasn't ready to say goodbye.
He suggested we get married and go together.
Insane. Utter madness.

We did it anyway.

Wait.
What?
I was married?

I was married – holy shit!

My 'friend's apartment' in Chippendale, the one where
Byron had walked me home after our first date.
That was my former apartment, our first home, where my
ex-husband still lived.
Lea was our cat. My cat.

We'd decided Joaquim would keep her.
Lea was happy there.
Plus, my new shared apartment in Mascot didn't allow pets.

The little white Mercedes snowball?
That was our first car.
After I'd lost my licence, Joaquim had driven me everywhere
I needed to go.

What happened to us?

Nothing dramatic, just the inevitable.
Barely out of school.
All passion, no plan.

Only known each other a few months before we exchanged
wedding bands and ate cake.
By the time we were furnishing our apartment in Sydney we
knew we weren't compatible.
The honeymoon was over before intermission.

Our mothers filed the divorce papers in Porto Alegre on our
behalf.
They cried for us as well.

What made me happy is that we'd stayed close friends after
the divorce.
Not a drop of bad blood.

Joaquim stayed in Sydney and made a wonderful life for
himself.
I was proud of him.
Grateful for his friendship.

He'd always been there for me.
I'd always been there for him.
And our cat.

He still mattered to me, even after I fell in love with Byron.
We'd kept in touch. Spoke all the time.

I found a trove of Joaquim's old emails and text messages.
His thoughtful and encouraging feedback on my idea to
create No Saints.

I valued his opinion.
I valued him.

So where had he been?
I'd not heard from Joaquim since my accident.

Did he not know?
How could he not know?

If ever I needed a friendly face, it was now.

I reached out.
At least I tried. Many times.
Joaquim didn't answer my calls or return my messages.

I called Mum.

She was so surprised she called Joaquim's mum to see if he
was okay.
Even Byron sent Joaquim messages letting him know how
much it would mean to me to hear from him.

Nothing.

Eventually, I found out Joaquim had a girlfriend who was jealous of the enduring connection he and I had shared. Joaquim told his mum to tell my mum to tell me that he wasn't able to see me or talk to me anymore.
However, he'd make a generous donation to my GoFundMe page.

There it was again.
Faux compassion.

I needed a friend.
Someone to talk to.
Someone I could trust.
I needed him.

Instead, he wrote a cheque.

Time is not money.
Time is humanity.

I hated myself for crying over such a pathetic cop-out.
For feeling so desperate. So unloved.
If I could, I would have crushed Joaquim's tiny heart with a pair of tweezers.

40.

Mining my hard drive.

Unearthing love letter after love letter.
Photo after photo.
Laughing, kissing, dancing.
In love. Loving life.
Everything that had gone wrong with Joaquim had gone
right with Byron.

We both had history.
Both had our quirks.

Byron was a bit of a hypochondriac.
I was a little needy.
He was cautious, I was adventurous.
But it worked.

We worked.

In our wedding photos, Joaquim and I looked perfect
together.
Too perfect.
Like cake-toppers with cheekbones.
Adorable but also, somehow, unreal.
A licensed image that pops up in a google search for 'cute
young couple getting married'.

Byron and I were the real thing.
Two adults.
With baggage.
Eyes wide open.

We'd lived together for a year before we started talking
about marriage.
Our relationship was stress-tested.

Our love had legs.
We were going the distance.

There were so many sweet and sincere references to us
getting married.
To starting a family.

I was ready to have Byron's children.
Ready for anything he wanted.
Anything.

In order to file my claim for compensation against the
Barcelona police department my lawyers required a
psychologist to complete a clinical evaluation of my brain
injury.

I didn't know where to begin.

Byron told me I was already seeing a psychologist before my
accident.
My jaw dropped. But I still wrote down the details.

Dr Donald Geliebter in Elizabeth Bay.
I made an appointment.

When I arrived at Dr Geliebter's office he acted like we were
old friends.
'Call me Don,' he said.
I had no memory of him.

Already off balance.
Don enjoyed keeping me there.

He liked to make little jokes.
Lots of little jokes.
About my altered appearance.
My wonky eye. The asymmetry of my face.
The way I walked.
Jokes about how little I had going on in my life post-accident.

It hurt.
All of it.

Nothing we discussed made me feel better about my
situation.
When the clinical evaluation was complete, I sent the file to
my lawyers without opening it.
I was too afraid to read it for fear of losing faith in myself.

Before I left his office, I asked Don about my previous visits.
I wanted to know when I'd started seeing him, and for how
long.
What we'd talked about.
Who'd referred me to him, and why.

Don wouldn't tell me.
Wouldn't even tell me why he wouldn't tell me.

As soon as I got home, I began combing through my
computer, my phone, my notebooks, my receipts.
Searching for clues.

Dr Geliebter had been recommended by Margo.
The unhappiness queen.

Terrific.

I'd begun seeing Don a few months after I left my job to
work fulltime on No Saints.

Starting a company from scratch is hard.
I thought I was ready.
Maybe I was.
But that didn't mean I knew what I was getting into.

It turned out Byron hadn't liked the idea of me quitting my job.
Felt it was premature to commit to a start-up.
But he stood by me.
Even as my money ran out.

Soon, I was financially dependent on him.
Which made me very unhappy.

In time, I was emotionally dependent on him as well.
I hated sitting at home on my own all the time.

Grinding away in isolation.
Waiting for things to take off.
Exhausted. Stressed.

Byron had a major investment project on the other side of
the country.
He worked late when he was home.
Very late.
And then he would be gone for days at a time.

I became miserable. Was miserable.
Started to spiral.

My depression manifested as an emotional black hole.
Groping for a lifeline of positivity and purpose, I became
more and more extreme about my vegan lifestyle.

Reason gave way to zealotry.
Angry. Judgemental. Fanatical.
The kind of person I never wanted to be.

Byron and I had a huge argument.
I accused him of abandoning me.
Never being around.
Always promising to come home and then breaking those
promises.

I was drowning. I wanted, needed him to prioritise me, us,
ahead of work.

Byron felt the opposite.
He said he loved his job.
Working late wasn't the problem.

I was the problem.

He'd lost half of his friends, he said, because I demanded he come home to me instead of socialising after office hours.

He felt we already spent too much time together.
I needed to find my own thing.
If he had to choose between me and his career, he'd choose his career.
Maybe we should just break up.

I spent the night at Grace's home.

Emotions were still running high the following weekend.
We fought again.

This time it was about starting a family.
About the child we didn't have.

I wanted to raise our children vegan.
Byron was open to this but wanted to be flexible.
He cherished the memories he had as a boy of going fishing with his dad, and wanted to do the same with our children one day.

I couldn't stand the idea of killing a fish.
Killing any animal for fun.
I was also furious that Byron hadn't read any of the research on the health benefits of a vegan diet, especially for young children.

Shouting. Tears.

I stayed with Olivia that night.

◊

It looked like Byron and I had reached the end of the road.
But somehow, we'd come back together.

We talked it out.
Didn't want to be apart.

Still loved each other.

◊

I read the clear-eyed notes in my journal.
As distant and knowing as scripture.

Relationship pros and cons.
I needed to be sure that Byron and I were compatible.

I'd confided in Grace that, as much as I loved Byron, I was
prepared to break up if we couldn't agree on key values as
the foundation for our life together.
For a family of our own.

I needed to know he would always stand by me.

Byron tried to spend more quality time at home.
Together time.
Put us first.

I put us first as well.
Owned my feelings.

I sought professional help to deal with stress, anxiety and
depression.

In time I saw how I had made veganism my religion.
I'd weaponised something gentle and kind and loving.
To prop myself up when I felt powerless and hopeless.
To direct my anger and fear away from myself.

Self-awareness sometimes tastes like shame.
It's humbling.
But also uplifting.
I wanted to be stronger.
I wanted to be better at loving others.

At loving myself.

A few months before our fateful trip to Europe, Byron and I
recommitted to each other.
We were going to make it work.

In a way, our summer holiday was a new beginning.
A honeymoon prelude.

41.

I found an overstuffed box of receipts and invoices.

I kept digging until I found something incongruous,
staggering.
A medical receipt for a pregnancy termination.

Just weeks before we started fighting.
I'd had an abortion.

I didn't understand.

Byron and I had wanted to have a child.
Children, plural.

Didn't we?

All life was sacred to me.
How was this possible?
Why would I ever ...

My mother was strong enough to be a sole parent.
Wasn't I?

Was my life at risk?
Was my baby dying, already dead?
What reason could be so compelling to make this choice?

When all I wanted, we wanted, was a home together.
Filled with life and love.

I needed to call Byron.
Ask him what had happened.
But I didn't.

Never called.
Never asked.

Not to spare his feelings.
But because his feelings didn't matter.

Women alone bear the burden of new life.
And all consequences of new life lost.
Physical, emotional, spiritual.

If it is deemed a crime, men are found innocent.
If it is a tragic accident of nature, women are judged.
Not consoled.

Guilty of wantonness.
Guilty of carelessness.
Guilty of heartlessness.
Guilty of agency over our own bodies.

But the intense agony of this discovery now.
At a time when I could barely look after myself.
Let alone a precious infant.

Knowing that motherhood was no longer a dream I could
put my arms around.

I sought comfort in empty promises.
Telling myself I could still have a family.
There were still possibilities.
Had to be.

If I continued to improve, one day I could adopt.
Would they let me adopt?
Not a baby, perhaps.
An older child.
Would they?

But the wound was so deep.

No one else knew or cared.
I alone grieved my loss unremembered.
I alone was present to offer bouquets of sorrow to my former self.

What she must have endured.
Would that I could hold her close.

How could I begin to tell her that another tragedy would make this terrible loss a blessing.
That being a childless woman was far better than being a motherless child.

How could she ever comprehend the vision of horror I described?

I had a vague half-memory of getting incredibly drunk the night before my abortion.

Dawning realisation that my depression and anxiety weren't entirely due to loneliness.
Or being overwhelmed by my new business.
There were far greater issues at play.

My body was still healing.
My heart was grieving.

Waking this nightmare stirred feelings of pain, regret, uncertainty.
But, ultimately, profound insight.

The epiphany cast everything Byron and I had fought about in a new light.
Harsher, yes.
And softer.

Great sorrow. Of course.
For what happened, and what might have been.
But also, gratitude.

Grateful to be in a modern country like Australia.
Where abortions are safe, legal and confidential.

But I could not walk this road twice.
I would not call Byron, or anyone, to help me relive this day.

For my own sake.

Not because I doubted my decision.
Quite the opposite.
I had faith in myself.
In the choices I'd made.

I replaced the receipt.
Closed the box.

42.

No one knows how the human brain works.
But I know how it feels when it's not working properly.

The inability to rein in impulses and new ideas.
Memory voids.
Random thoughts and impressions catalogued without
context or priority.

Simple, crucial details, hovering just out of reach.
Dust motes dancing in sunlight.

As my brain began to repair itself, I started having vivid,
hyperdetailed dreams.
Old friends, former colleagues, news headlines.
Everything was so clear, so real.
Sharp colour and focus beyond the edge of memory.

I saw David again.
Recovering from his stroke in his hospital bed.
I was there, back in his room.

In waking life I'd lost my sense of smell, but in my dream
the medical-grade disinfectant on every surface was
overwhelming.
The ammonia filled my nostrils, made my eyelids flicker.

One night I witnessed a murder.

A young Brazilian woman, Cecília.
Long dark hair, beautiful smile.
Surprised in her own apartment.
Terror and rage.
Slender throat crushed by the hands of her ex-boyfriend.
Rocks and river stones shoved into the pockets of her
clothes to weight her down.
Her lifeless body floating in a brackish current towards
Sydney Harbour.
The murderer fleeing to Rio de Janeiro.

The next day I called Grace.
She told me it wasn't a prophecy or a movie.
This had really happened, in 2018.
All of it.
Exactly as I described.

The killer had been arrested by civil police officers in Rio de
Janeiro, while hiding out with relatives.

Olivia had known the victim personally.
They'd even worked together.

We'd all moved in vaguely similar circles.
Cecília's office was just blocks from mine.

Grace told me that, at the time, she, Olivia and I had talked a great deal about this horrible crime.

I called Olivia to ask her about Cecília.
Never heard back.
Still avoiding me, it seemed.

But the fact that my brain had just screened this memory in high definition as I slept, seemed very strange.
I liked to think, to hope, that it was a side effect of severed axons finding new ways to reconnect isolated memories.

My brain was slowly but surely rewiring itself.

There were other side effects.
Some were terrifying.

I lived alone now.
For the first time in ten years.
Since before I married Joaquim.

One Friday evening, a bomb silently exploded inside my head.

Excruciating pain.
Starting between my eyes and stabbing backwards.
Somewhere deep inside my skull.
Intense and dizzying.
I fell to the floor in agony.

Could barely see.
Or speak.
Groping blindly for my phone.
Called my mum.
No idea what time of day or night it was in Caxias do Sul.

I couldn't fully describe what was happening, but I needed
help.

My mother called the only three people in Australia she
believed I could count on.

Olivia. Didn't answer.
Byron. Out of town.
Grace. Apologised but couldn't come over.

Mum was beside herself.
She and I were thinking the same thing.
Felicia.
I had Felicia's exact symptoms.

I didn't want to die in front of my cat.

I stumbled to my bedroom and curled up in the foetal
position on the bed until I passed out.
Slept all day.

Headache so severe and blinding that I could barely move.
Couldn't even answer my phone.
On the two occasions I tried to eat or drink, I vomited.
Immediately.

I can only imagine how distressing this was for my mother.
She kept calling to check on my condition, but I couldn't even hold the phone.
Repeatedly messaged my three closest friends to come to my aid.
No one responded.

Byron finally received my mum's messages.
Cancelled his weekend and came back early.
After letting himself into my apartment he helped me drink some açaí juice and drove me to the nearest emergency room.

I didn't have an aneurysm.
Huge relief.

But I could expect more of these debilitating headaches.

Injured areas within my brain had become hypersensitive.
When triggered, they would blast out pain signals that would then be amplified by other parts of my brain.

It felt like a monster with long, hot claws scooping out the contents of my skull.
I was prescribed heavy-duty painkillers.
Additional medications would reduce the frequency and intensity of these horrific migraines.
But there was nothing that would prevent them completely.

The monster was here to stay.

43.

I hadn't seen Olivia for ages.

She didn't invite me to her birthday party.
But then, Covid had shrunk social events for safety reasons.

Also, no one invited me to parties anymore.

I bought Olivia a birthday present anyway.
We made plans to catch up.
Plans that she postponed.
More than once.

When we finally met for lunch, it was clear Olivia didn't
want to be there.
She accepted my gift graciously.
But she didn't eat, had very little to say, and left early.

That evening I caught up with Grace and told her about the
lunch date that wasn't.

Olivia was the one who'd supposedly slept with my
boyfriend while I was in hospital.
I'd put this aside to maintain our friendship.
So why was she being horrible to me?

Grace said she'd speak to Olivia, and smooth things over.

I'm not sure what happened after that.
Or what Grace said.
But Olivia blocked me.
Never spoke to me. Ever again.

Traumatic brain injury is an invisible disability.

According to medical textbooks, the most serious effects are loss of motor function, impaired cognitive function, limited comprehension, emotional volatility and slurred speech.
All of that is true.

But, in my experience, the greatest casualty of a brain injury is friendship.
The defining symptom is loneliness.

I came home to watch my friends leave me.
One by one.

Byron finally admitted he'd had an affair.

He didn't name the woman, or women, but he apologised for hurting me, and for the upsetting messages Mum and I had received.

He confessed he'd started seeing someone, sleeping with someone, after he returned to Sydney.
Following the last time he visited me in Spain.
For Christmas.

When he'd told the woman he wasn't able to commit to her because he was still emotionally invested in me, she became furious.
That's when she started angrily messaging me, my mum.
Our whole extended family at one stage.
Tacky AF.

In his mind, Byron believed our romantic relationship had ended in Barcelona.
The woman he'd loved was gone forever.
Our future was over.

That's what he'd told himself.
That's what he'd told his friends.

And his new lovers.

Wounded.
Angry, too.
Furious.
At Byron's romantic betrayal.
And the notion that I was dead to him when I was very much alive.

Not enough time had passed to make this easy for me.

But.
I forgave him.

Byron had suffered with me.
He wasn't the same person he was before Barcelona.
Not anymore.

My accident had fractured him too.

He'd soaked up a lot of trauma.
I knew that.
I took some responsibility for this as well.

I also understood his pain.
Far better than he understood mine.

Byron had crushed my heart to crimson grease beneath his heel.
But he had also genuinely been there for me since I returned home to Bondi.

I hated being pitied.
Treated like a dysfunctional child.
Especially by someone I'd hoped to marry and have a family with.

But, other than my mum, no one had done more than Byron to help me cope with post-accident life.

He encouraged me.

Protected me.

Defended me to my critics.

He took me shopping and ensured I had everything I needed.

Explained and re-explained countless things I'd forgotten.

He was my handyman and my next-of-kin emergency contact.

Made sure my money was safe and my bills were paid.

Fought for justice on my behalf.

He even let me keep my home office at his apartment.

Byron checked in on me when no one else cared.

He kept me company when no one else would.

He forgave my embarrassing gaffes and angry outbursts
when no one else did.

And he asked for nothing in return.

Byron did all this out of love.

Or maybe guilt.

Was he merely punishing himself?

I couldn't begin to know.

But he had been my rock.

I wanted to get over him so badly.

But I was so grateful he was in my life.

His finance bros were right for once.

Byron was a saint.

Albeit an imperfect one.

He deserved my sympathy and gratitude.

More importantly, my initial instincts were accurate.

Byron was a good man.

A very good man.

He just wasn't the man for me.

44.

I also knew what it felt like to crave the comfort and pleasure
of human touch.
Especially when you were in emotional pain.
Feeling alone. Left behind.
Unseen.

One of my rehab psychologists, a sex therapist, asked me
about my romantic goals.
My sexual desires.
I answered as best I could.

Yes. I would like to meet someone special.
Yes. I was open to a serious relationship.
Yes. I missed physical intimacy.

But when she started asking about what my ideal partner
and future relationship might look like, the greater truth was
revealed.

I wanted everything I had lost.
I wanted to meet Byron all over again.

Covid restrictions, limited mobility, communication
challenges.
A skeletal social network.
Meeting people was hard.

Finding love, all but impossible.

I tried dating apps.
They'd worked before.

Online window shopping for love was a fun way to pass the lonely hours.
Chatting with men I'd never meet, let alone date.

In the end, this futile exercise became an ersatz English class.

My spelling and grammar improved.
My ability to find love did not.

I searched and searched.
But couldn't find another Byron.

I wondered if this part of my life was over.
Another casualty of my traumatic brain injury.
Exile in a psychosexual desert.

I was listening to Life Uncut, my favourite podcast.
Their guest was a woman who'd opened a swingers' club in Annandale.
Twenty minutes from Bondi.

A private club for, ahem, open-minded adults.
So creepy.
But also, in that moment, kind of intriguing.

Old me would have run a mile.
New me wasn't so easily scared off.

It's not uncommon for those with brain injuries to become
hypersexual.
Their lack of inhibitions can further isolate them from
family and friends, at a time when they need them most.

In my case, I just felt incredibly lonely.
Physically and emotionally dislocated.

Byron was supposed to sweep me up in his strong arms.
We'd make love, get married.
Fill our home with kittens and babies.

Instead, I'd been abandoned.
Walled up inside a romantic vacuum.
An untouchable.

My vagina had been buried alive.

Invisibility is a form of death.

I wanted to be seen.
Longed for the affirmation of desire.

Neither reckless nor shameless.
I didn't tell my mum what I was planning.
She would have understood, I'm sure.

But she would have made a pained face of disapproval that,
as we say in Brazil, looks like '*cão chupando manga*'.
A *dog sucking on a mango.*

I was ready to take some risks.
The world left me no other choice.
This or nothing.

I bought a ticket online.
Put on a cute skirt. Shoes I wouldn't fall over in.
And went to the Annandale club for drinks.

The venue's grubby exterior did not reassure.
If only by contrast, the interior was a pleasant surprise.

Clean, safe. Nightclub stylish.
Courteous staff. Great music.
Chilled champagne.
Zero pressure.

I didn't hate it.

I'd expected hungry-eyed entitled men.
But there weren't many of those.
And they were easily waved off.
Consent was everything.

Most of the crowd that night were couples.
Trying to spice up their love life.
Have a little fun.

All ages, all shapes, all sizes.
People feeling sexy.
Trying to feel sexy.

What struck me though, was how many people were like me.
A little damaged.
A little hopeful.

Wise to their own desires.
Desperate enough to be brave.
Brave enough to be vulnerable.

Aching. Searching.
Yearning for affection and intimacy.
The most beautiful human connection.

One that, for whatever reason, we'd been denied.

I chose a man with a kind face.
No promises were made or broken.

It was honest.
Liberating.
Empowering.

After the whole world had tried to break me.
I was still a woman in my prime.

I was alive.
I was awake.

45.

Months, so many months.
Searching through my notes.

Exquisitely neat, ordered notes.
Numbers, designs, flowcharts, material research, marketing
strategies.
Painstaking detail.

Written by someone who cared about everything.
Knew everything.

I saw what my purpose was.
My plans for No Saints were everywhere.

Still wanted it.
So badly.
I just didn't know how to make it happen.

Former me understood every step needed to start her
company.
She'd won business scholarships, had become an expert on
and understood every aspect of every operation.
I was in awe of her.
Envied her.

I was afraid I could never like myself as much as I loved who
I used to be.

New me was lost.

I could understand the basic elements.
But my creative energy and power of concentration had been
shattered and scattered by a speeding police car.
Regathering the mental momentum needed for No Saints to
reach the tipping point again seemed beyond me.

Byron had put in seed capital.
But he assumed he'd lost his money and his girlfriend at the
same time.
My other angel investors held a similar view.

Cutting their losses.

I was the brand.
The brand was me.
Without me driving No Saints, from concept sketches to
final stitch, our product line was discontinued before it even
launched.

My mentors wouldn't talk to me.
Or maybe they did, once or twice.
Until they realised I couldn't remember what they'd said.
Kept asking them the same questions.

In the early stages of recovery, brain damage, stupid, drunk
and crazy all sound the same.

But only one of those conditions applied to me.
Most of the time.

The volume of work I'd invested in No Saints was
monumental.
This had been a huge part of my life.

It was my life.

Grace tried to lift me out of misery quicksand.
She listened to my litany of losses.

I'd come so close.
So close.
Having it all.

But then.
It had been taken away.
All of it. Everything.

My mind, my body.
I couldn't smell the perfume of spring, or my cat's litter box.
My head and face had changed shape.
My ears and eyes were no longer aligned.
Reading made me seasick.
It hurt to walk. To lie down. To breathe.

I'd lost my lover. My home.
Everything we'd dreamed of together.

The engagement ring, the wedding album, the trimesters,
first day of kindergarten, family vacations.
Lifelong friends who'd become our family as well.

Sometimes, I caught Byron looking at me like he used to.
Just a glance.
Quick as a field of flowers sliding past the window of a
speeding train.
I was the beautiful woman he loved.

And then it was gone.

I was no longer beautiful, his lover, or even a woman.
But a broken thing.
To be calmed and pitied.

I'd lost almost all my friends.

The cupcake savagery of rich bitches didn't bother me.
But my dearest friends, my truest friends.
Sisters to the end.

We'd shared everything.
Been there for each other.
Yet they'd abandoned me as well.

Not for anything I'd done with ill intent.
But because, for a time, my brain injury had made me too
loud, too erratic, too confrontational, too unfiltered.
I'd embarrassed them.

I wanted to scream that I was sorry, that this wasn't really
me.
That this was my brain healing, this was only temporary.
But, then I'd just be screaming again.
And they hated that.

I'd lost my job, my career.

I rang my former boss.
The one who'd often called me his star employee.
I asked him if he'd let me come back, even part-time.
I'd work for free until I'd relearned everything.
He said they wouldn't have any vacancies for two years.
A polite way of letting me know I was unemployable.

I lost my innate gift for mathematics.
Numbers were hard now, elusive, shifty.
I needed to use a calculator for perhaps the first time in my
life.

I'd lost my ability to soak up new knowledge.
Academic all-star to dunce.

I signed up for a university course in marketing.
To push myself, to accelerate growth and healing.
Make use of the time I no longer spent socialising.

Within an hour, half an hour, I withdrew from the class.
Too many words, too many diagrams, too fast, too much.

The faculty took pity on me. Refunded my money.
I couldn't even begin to begin.
Sisyphus on roller skates.

And now, I'd lost No Saints.
The last glittering relic of my former life.
My purpose.

The only remaining thing that was mine.

Without this, every dream had been stolen.
Everything that my best self ever cared about had come to
nothing.
Gone.

And what made it unbearable was that all the heavy lifting
was in the past.
My vision mapped and codified as business plans and
blueprints.
Production engine forged and fuelled.

I'd bent retail gravity to my will.
Aligned my own stars. Hand over hand.

It was all there.
Everything was ready.
But I hadn't done it.
And now I never would.

I wanted to cry.

Tears didn't come easily.
Dry sobs. Goat noises.
I couldn't do anything right anymore.

Grace hugged me till I was quiet.
My breathing slowed.

Then she took my hand.
Led me through my own apartment.
To a door I'd never noticed.
Didn't remember.
Turned the handle.

A small room.
Filled with eco-friendly designer shoeboxes.
Floor to ceiling.

Each box cradled a beautiful pair of No Saints shoes.

The same gorgeous shoes that Byron had given me when I
returned to Sydney.

The same shoes scattered around my office at Byron's apartment.
Shoes I'd worn out countless times.
The shoes I was wearing at that very moment.

No Saints existed.

◊

I'd already built the ethical fashion company of my dreams.
I'd launched my first line of shoes before we went overseas.

Byron and I hadn't just gone on a European holiday to rebuild our relationship.
We were celebrating No Saints as well.

It was still early days, but people loved the shoes.
Sales had even picked up when I'd had my accident.
A small but meaningful way for customers to show they cared.

Grace and other close friends had done their best to keep the company alive in my absence.
They'd personally sold my shoes at vegan markets across Sydney.

Of course, production and sales had dropped off by now.
Dormant for more than a year.

Just like me.

But if I could wake up.
So could my company.

◇

Grace smiled.
Her eyes glistened.
'You did it,' she said.

◇

Kissing a high-speed police car had not brought me luck.

Nothing had turned out quite the way I'd hoped.
And yet, somehow, it had turned out the way I'd planned.

I'd quit my corporate job.
I was out of a relationship that I now knew could not go the distance.
I was on track to become an Australian citizen.
I'd started the ethical fashion company that represented my purpose in life.
I was doing all the things the doctors said I'd never do again.
And there was more to come.

Even if my mind and body were broken, I was still alive.
My dream was alive.

'*Eu consigo tudo que eu quero.*'
'*I get everything I want.*'

46.

I wish my story ended in a small room filled with shoeboxes.
A wondrous moment of epiphany.
The golden light of my best friend's smile.

But it doesn't.

Months passed.

For my mum and me, the anonymous online bullying
continued.

> **Caroline is alone and will end
> up getting involved with drugs,
> she could be raped, she could be
> abused. You have to look after her!**
>
> **Caroline, go back to Brazil. Byron
> needs to move on with his life. He
> deserves to be happy too.**

I was trying my best to get No Saints back up and running.
Exhilarating. Exhausting.

No one wanted to invest in a company run by a young
woman with a traumatic brain injury.

Without additional support, I couldn't hire more staff to help me, ramp up marketing or production.

Despite the difficulty.
Hard work. Stress.
This was still my purpose.

There was great joy in that.

Mum and I talked every day.
Byron checked in on me regularly.
But Grace had become a little distant.

Partly, Grace was annoyed that I was annoyed when she treated me like a child.
In her mind, she was being considerate.
But it sure felt like gaslighting to me.

Having a brain injury impacts your ability to read others.
You can seem oblivious.

I reminded myself that Grace was entitled to be busy with her own life.
She'd also moved.

So, we didn't see each other as often as either of us would have liked.
Certainly not as much as I would've liked.

We kept making plans to catch up.
Somehow, they never happened.
Grace always postponed or cancelled at the last minute.

It was frustrating.
Disappointing.

◇

My horrific accident and torturous recovery had taken a
terrible toll on my mum.

Long-distance mothering meant constant worry,
helplessness.
Especially when she kept receiving anonymous hate messages
about me.

Yet, despite these corrosive forces, she respected my wish to
be independent and encouraged me constantly.

That's true love.

By the time she'd returned to Brazil, Mum could barely use
her hands.
Stress had triggered her autoimmune disease, resulting in
crippling rheumatoid arthritis.

Brazil's response to Covid was one of the worst in the world.
Which is really saying something.
Politicians refused to act, or even acknowledge the pandemic
was real.
Hospitals were overwhelmed.

Many collapsed.
Those that remained open became death traps for
immunocompromised people, like my mum.

Mum took what medication she could at home.
She tried to rest.
Qelbes did all he could to ease her suffering.

But the inflammation in her joints only got worse.
Mum's immune system was attacking the rest of her body.
It became unbearable. Undiluted agony.

If untreated, her bones would be eaten away, her hands
deformed.
Wasted fingers twisting into the talons of a dead bird.
She'd never work again.

Life's simplest tasks would become all but impossible.
I already knew something about that.
And I wouldn't wish it on my worst enemy.

The risk of the inflammation spreading to Mum's heart and
lungs increased exponentially.
She had no choice but to seek specialist help.

Qelbes drove her the two hours to Porto Alegre.

There were no Covid vaccines in Brazil at that time.
Mum and Qelbes took every possible precaution.
Only taking their masks off just the once.

To eat a small meal at an open-air restaurant.

Other diners started coughing.
Waiters were coughing.
A few days later, Mum started coughing.
A little.
Then a lot.

At first, Mum claimed she had allergies.
It was just allergies.

But then the headache gripped her head like a vice.
Breathing took more effort.
A doctor confirmed she had Covid.

With Mum's autoimmune disease it was far too risky to go
to a medical facility.
If she walked in through the doors of a hospital, it was almost
certain her lifeless body would be wheeled out a few days later.

She isolated at home and received remote treatment.

Qelbes contracted Covid as well.
Fortunately, his case was not as severe, and he was able to
care for Mum as he recovered.
It can't have been easy.

Thankfully, the intensity of his symptoms was inversely
proportional to the love he felt for my mother.

Qelbes' daughter, my stepsister, is a doctor.
She called in a favour from a virologist she knew.

The virologist agreed to monitor Mum's condition via
phone, so she wouldn't have to be moved.
However, the course of antibiotics and corticosteroids he
prescribed couldn't halt her rapid decline.

Over the following week, Mum's oxygen levels dropped lower.
And lower.
She grew weaker by the day.
Couldn't keep her eyes open.
Eventually, Qelbes was unable to wake her up.

The worst possible option became our only option.
Qelbes took her to the hospital.

When oxygen levels fall below 70 per cent it becomes life
threatening.
Mum was at 50 per cent.

She had Covid pneumonia.
The tiny air sacs in her lungs were filled with pus and fluid.
The doctors put her on oxygen.
They gave her every medication they could think of.

We were told her recovery was unlikely.
To prepare for the worst.

Paulo Gustavo, Mum's favourite comedian, had just died.
He'd had the same symptoms.

It was time to say goodbye.

I felt useless on the far side of the world.
Frightened and helpless.

The thought of losing my mother was –
I couldn't even begin to –

I needed Grace.
I needed to see my best friend.
My only true friend.

I called her.
Thank god she answered this time.
Said she would drop everything.

We made plans to meet up for dinner. That night.

But something came up at home. She had to postpone.
So, it became lunch, the following day.
Grace postponed again.
We settled on breakfast on the weekend.
Saturday. No, Sunday worked better for her.

I reserved a table for us at The Nine.
Our favourite Mediterranean café.
Grace promised to pick me up on the way.
Save me the walk.

I woke up early on the morning of.
Fed Sundy, got dressed.

Then I waited. Waited.
Waited.

Grace didn't show.

I was hungry for breakfast and her company.
I messaged her.
'Where are you?'

An hour later, she messaged me back.
She had slept in. Running super late.
So sorry.

'No worries,' I said. 'Let's call it brunch instead.'

Grace wasn't open to this idea.
She was playing tennis at noon.
Didn't want to feel full.

I love watching tennis, so I suggested I join her there.
Then we could grab a bite afterwards. Catch up properly.

No, she just couldn't do it.
Wouldn't do it.

Grace said she was free on Thursday, the following week.

My heart felt like a hot stone.
If I didn't vent, my eyebrows were going to catch fire.

Literally the only person I could call was Byron.

My unsuspecting ex was eating a late breakfast at Up South
Bondi.
We used to go there every weekend.
Our local café when we lived together.
Still his.

Byron was dining alone and said he was happy for me to join
him.
Or at least, he tried to make it sound like he was happy.
Which I appreciated.

My balance wasn't great to begin with.
And I was all worked up as I walked to the café.
I tripped over a driveway. Fell heavily on the concrete footpath.

Bleeding knuckles.
Bruises.
Byron helped me patch myself up before I ate.

Scrambled tofu, fried mushrooms and hummus.
Coffee.
Thank heavens for coffee.

Started feeling better.

Byron knew about Mum.
He expressed his genuine concern and sympathy.
There wasn't anything much he could say or do, but his
kindness helped.
A lot.

Following our breakfast farewell, I started walking home.
Just short of my apartment I stopped.

I didn't want to be alone.
Couldn't be alone that day.

I was too ashamed to call Byron again.
Then I saw on Instagram that Margo, of all people, was nearby.

Just five minutes' walk away.

Upgrading her tan at the Bondi Icebergs.
Bondi's legendary lifesaver swimming-club-cum-sceney-hang for sun-worshipping beautiful people.

I swallowed my pride and messaged Margo, asking if I could join.
Casually begging.
That's how desperate I was.

I don't know if Margo meant to say yes, or was too shocked to say no.

Quick pitstop at home.
Threw a denim skirt over a black bikini.
Slipped on some pale pink flip-flops.

Headed over.

Treading with extra care this time.
I made it safely to the footpath beside Bondi Beach park.
And down the hillside stairs to the Icebergs.

At swimming pool level, I waded through a mass of
glistening, semi-naked bodies.
Writhing and lolling about in the sun like oiled-up semi-
inebriated seals.

I caught sight of Margo, who was far closer than I'd thought.
She spotted me at the exact same moment.
We were both surprised.
I half-stepped back to wave hello and slipped-tumbled
straight into the children's pool.
As I fell, my right leg snagged on the pool's unyielding
concrete lip
Gashed from knee to ankle.

Every now and then, a violent storm tosses a passing shark
into the ocean-fed swimming pools.
That's how it looked as I slapped and floundered in an
expanding crimson cloud of my own blood.

Margo leapt to my rescue and was joined by a chiselled
crush of Aussie lifeguards.
She stayed with me while I received first aid from the oldest
man to ever wear speedos.

The wound was ugly-messy.

Painful, but not critical.
More of a deep graze really.

I took a photo of my bloody leg and sent it to Grace.
I added a dark joke about how the day had gone horribly
wrong since she had slept in.
We'd missed our breakfast date, and now I was being
bandaged.
The good news was that I already had a limp.
Plus, my modelling aspirations began and ended in my
teens, when my proud aunt put me on a poster for a local
cosmetics store.
One more scar wasn't going to matter.

So … no harm done.
LOL.

Margo kindly helped me walk home before returning to her
sunbathing.

I'm sure my blood being sprayed across a dozen beach
towels, and tinting the children's pool water rust pink, was
just what she needed to revise her opinion of how stressful it
was to socialise with me since my accident.

I wasn't invited to join any new WhatsApp groups.

Byron came to my apartment that evening to help me re-dress the wound, so that it wouldn't stick to my bed sheets.
Such a good man.

◇

My mum was choking and gasping into a ventilator when she received a photo of my bloody leg, accompanied by a cruel, anonymous message.

> **This is what is happening to**
> **Caroline when you're not around.**
> **You need to be here.**

I'd only shared that photo with one person.

◇

Grace's toxic message didn't aid Mum's recovery.
But she refused to die.
Wouldn't give Grace the satisfaction.
Wouldn't leave her disabled daughter behind for something as trivial as death.

After a few critical days in hospital, Mum turned the corner.
She was able to go home, where her convalescence would be far safer.

I waited till Mum was feeling better, and her strength had returned.
Then I brought up the mean message that could only have come from Grace.

I'd had time to put all the pieces together.
Identified all the anonymous hate messages that Mum and I
had received from Grace since I returned to Australia.

The evidence was conclusive.
But I still struggled to accept that my best friend had been
behind this vicious campaign all along.
Couldn't understand her motive.

Mum knew more than I did.
As always.

It was Grace who'd first approached Mum, ostensibly on
Byron's behalf, to discourage her from letting me return to
Australia.
She was the one who'd told Mum and Qelbes that I should
not be allowed to hold Byron back.
She'd told Mum, and probably Byron as well, that he didn't
owe me any loyalty, as we weren't a married couple.
Not in her eyes.
Not officially.

Grace made it clear to Mum, and anyone who would listen,
that Byron had suffered enough already.
He should be allowed to move on.
My injuries were a tragedy, but I was beyond salvage.
It would be unforgivable to ruin Byron's life as well.

Grace told Mum that she had been to see Byron's parents, to
discuss how I should be kept away from their son.

However, it was clear that Byron's mum had not agreed with whatever abandonment strategy Grace had laid out.
Embeth continued to call me.
She'd frequently check on my progress. Share her love and support.

I realised now that Grace had been undermining me for well over a year.

I thought I knew how to suffer.
But this was a completely new type of hurt.

A sinkhole forming in my chest.

I asked Mum why she hadn't told me all this before.
Her reasons were as simple as the situation was complex.

She knew me well enough to know that I wanted control over my own fate.
Brain damage or no, I wasn't a passenger.
She still trusted me to make my own decisions.

She said that Grace's first messages appeared shortly after we'd been unable to return to Sydney from Barcelona.
In those early days of my recovery I wasn't even capable of understanding.

Also, Mum simply never believed anybody could be so cruel.
There had to be a misinterpretation.

Perhaps Grace's grasp of Portuguese wasn't what it used
to be.

Mum hoped by staying silent and not doing anything to
create conflict between me and my best friend that, in time,
we would re-establish our friendship.
Grace's inherent goodness would win out.
As it had with Byron.

But it didn't. It hadn't.

Grace had betrayed me. Again, and again.
She'd told my grieving boyfriend I'd been planning to break
up with him.
Sabotaged my friendship with Olivia.
Pushed me out of our social circle.

Tried to bury my memory in a shallow grave.

All to protect Byron from the horrific burden that was me.
At least, that was how she saw it.

On one level, Grace kicking me when I was down was
unspeakably cruel.
Motivated by fear, ignorance, jealousy.
Who knows?

But her poisonous strategy was also comically absurd.
Thanks to my traumatic brain injury, alienating friends was
my superpower.
I didn't need her help.

◇

I was crushed by Grace's betrayal.
But I found the courage to confront her.

At first, she denied sending the messages.
Denied everything.
But the evidence was clear.

She raved and babbled about how she was trying to help me.
That she'd done so much for me.
She'd kept No Saints going, she said, even at the cost of her
own career.
She only cared about my wellbeing.
Byron's wellbeing.

And, besides, she had merely said what everybody else was
already thinking.
I needed to be looked after properly, by my family.
Not dumped in a foreign land to fend for myself.

But I hadn't been dumped anywhere, by anybody.

My mother had nursed me back to health over many
months, years.
I'd begged her to let me be more independent.
She didn't leave me until I'd demonstrated I was able to look
after myself.

I knew the enormous challenges I'd be facing.
I'd embraced them all.
My mind and body were becoming stronger by the day.

This was my home.
I had a boyfriend I'd lived with for years.
I had a huge social network of amazing friends.
They were my family too.

Or at least, they used to be.

Until Grace had made it her mission to isolate me.
A broken girl.
To destroy everything that mattered to me.

And for what?
To save a grown man from his own decency?

Like all cartoon villains, Grace had failed.

The one friend who refused to abandon me in the end was
Byron.
The very person Grace was so desperate to shield.

Realising she was caught in her own lies, Grace's mask
slipped.
Her parting shot was jagged and spiteful.

She made it clear that, in her eyes, I was broken beyond
repair.
The new me was nothing like the person she'd been close
friends with.

Her final act of kindness, she said, was to try to remember
me how I used to be.
Not how I was now.

Then she blocked me.
Blocked my mum.
Vanished us with a flick of her thumb.

Grace and I never spoke to each other.
Never saw each other.
Ever again.

> *Say you'll never let me go.*
> *Say you'll never let me go.*

Prologue Redux

When I was seventeen, I was invited to apply for a full
scholarship at the Instituto Tecnológico de Aeronáutica
(ITA); Brazil's answer to MIT.
Arguably the most prestigious aerospace engineering
university in the country.
One of the best in the world.

The thought of completing a civil-aeronautical engineering
degree at ITA was thrilling.
Then, the chill of doubt set in.
Icy fingers clutched my teenage heart.

The best and brightest students in Brazil would be
competing for the same opportunity.
Less than 1 per cent of invited candidates would be accepted.

What if I didn't get in?
What if I wasn't good enough?

I could not abide the tiniest blemish on my sterling academic
record.

In the end, I didn't even sit the ITA entry exams.
Paralysed by my fear of failure.
My obsession with perfection prevented me from being the
best version of myself.

I slammed a door in my own face.

Being broken cured me of perfectionism.

I would never be perfect again.
That was painfully obvious.
To Grace. To everyone.

But I finally saw that I was never perfect.
I'd never met a perfect person.
And I never would.

Yes, I am broken.
More than that, I have broken free from everything that
would hold me back.

I would never again let myself become prisoner to the
unrealistic expectations of others.
Or my own.

Trauma should not be gift-wrapped.

A cloud's silver lining is just a trick of the light.
Not a measure of the storm brewing in its belly.
The tempest unseen.

Pain invisible.

Being me is harder now.
I hurt.

I forget.
I obsess.
I'm impatient.
I procrastinate.
The constant agony of navigating a fractured mind.

Barbed wire and molasses.

And yet there is beauty to be found in the way fate reshapes
us.
I am stronger for my scars.
I fear less.
Love more.

My mum told me I was a very emotional child.
Cried when anything went wrong.

Tears don't come so easily now.

But laughter does.

Within every body of water there is a small fish swimming
upside down.
Sick, injured.
Just different.

The little upside-down fish doesn't seek your pity.
She is immune to criticism and cruel jokes.
The suggestions that she should be put out of her misery.
Tossed aside. Thrown away.

Maybe one day she will swim just like all the other fish.
Maybe she won't.

Either way.
She is where she is meant to be.
Doing what she was born to do.
As best she can.

She will never stop.
And she will go far.
Blink and you'll lose sight of her.

Ours is a water planet after all.

There are pieces of me that I may never find, never recover.
My search will continue.
But I am enough as I am.

I have the sleepless desire to live a life of positive
consequence.
And I possess the determination to make it so.
Greater than genius.
Greater than beauty.
Greater than opportunity.
Greater than any gift but one.

My mother's love.

Becoming an Australian citizen was a bittersweet moment.
Three times, I'd fought my way to these golden shores.

Such a beautiful country.
Beautiful people.

But.
It didn't feel like home anymore.

I am a work in progress.
Fourteen surgeries complete.
Three to go.
Maybe more.

A life half over, yet barely begun.

So much living to do.
So much to learn and relearn.
Memories to reclaim.
Memories to make.

New friends to meet.
Old friends to rediscover.

I'm alive and awake.

To my eyes reopened, so much is beautiful and new.
Every smile is a first smile.
Every kiss, a first kiss.

I went to Byron's apartment to collect a few things from my old office.

Half-hidden on a bookshelf, I found my black and white sundress, from Spain.
Folded up neatly. Sleeved inside a plastic bag.
Still tie-dyed with my blood.

The Barcelona police, perhaps the paramedics, or a nurse, returned the dress to Byron at the hospital.
While I lay naked on an operating table.

I was taken aback by this gruesome memento.
'Why didn't you throw it away?' I asked Byron.

'I will,' he answered.
'But not yet.'
'I'm not ready to let go.'

But I was.

The best shoes in the world are handmade in Portugal.

I bought two plane tickets to Lisbon.

One for Sundy.
One for me.

Acknowledgements

While fighting to reclaim control over my mind and body the greatest challenge I faced was being locked out.
Many of my closest friends, former colleagues and even members of my own extended family were annoyed and embarrassed by the new, unfiltered me.
After a few awkward encounters, they no longer gave me the time of day.
Let alone time to heal.

What I needed most was meaningful human interaction to practise listening, speaking, relearning social cues and, most crucially, to feel safe, loved and included.
Instead, I was ignored, uninvited and abandoned.
I later learned that my experience of rejection and isolation is painfully common for those living with a brain injury.

Telling my story was extremely difficult.
It hurt every time I forced myself to confront the deep pain of my recent past.
Reliving my lowest moments made me weep, gave me nightmares.

But it felt like the only way to make the world unforget me.

My hope is that others who have suffered a brain injury will feel seen and heard because of what I have shared.

That their friends and loved ones will be more patient with them as they navigate a long and difficult recovery journey.

That people will realise a traumatic brain injury is more than a broken mind. It's also a broken heart, and a broken life.

◇

BTG and I would like to thank our Australian literary agent, Jeanne Ryckmans, from Key People Literary Management, and Sophie Hamley, from Hachette Australia, for bringing our book to life.

I would like to personally acknowledge all the wonderful people who didn't walk away, starting with my stepfather, Qelbes, who has been so kind, loving and funny ever since the day he entered my life.

I wish to express my sincere appreciation to Byron and his caring family who, after everything we've been through, continue to show me great kindness.

My Aunt Jane and Aunt Cátia both flew around the world to be by my side. Candice Pickworth Dolby generously reached out via Instagram to share invaluable and hard-won recovery advice and encouragement, even though we'd never met.

Officer Ágata, from Barcelona's Guàrdia Urbana Accident Prevention and Investigation Unit, went above and beyond her duty as a police officer to show my family and me tremendous compassion. I'm also indebted to Professor Denise Lindstrom Bandeira, my wonderful former academic advisor who, eleven years after I graduated from university, is once again my mentor and champion, reigniting my passion for learning.

I offer my heartfelt gratitude to the gifted medical and rehabilitation professionals in Barcelona, Curitiba and Sydney, who saved my life and taught me how to walk and talk again. Dr Gerardo Conesa Bertrán, the Chief of Neurosurgery and Director of the Teknon Neuroscience Institute, performed miracle after miracle to keep me alive.

He was also an enormous support to my mother – nothing was too much trouble for him. Also, his hair looks incredible. Seriously.

And my amazing Brazilian speech pathologist, Andréia Estér Puhl, moved heaven and earth for me so many times.

Even after I moved back to Australia, she would get up early and stay up late in Passo Fundo, so I could speak to her via video chat from Sydney. There were days when Andréia was the only person who'd listen to what I had to say.

I am so grateful to Fernanda and Marcelo, at the Brazilian Consulate in Barcelona, who worked around the clock to clear a path through seemingly endless diplomatic roadblocks to arrange my safe repatriation, during the height of Covid, when I was most vulnerable.

Above all, I wish to publicly thank my mother, Juceli, for her unwavering love and support throughout this incredibly difficult time.

My greatest life regret is the terrible pain and distress my accident and recovery caused her.

Her life was shattered, just as mine was, and yet she selflessly put aside her own needs and dreams, again and again, to focus on mine.

I cannot easily express how much my mother's sacrifice has meant to me, or how her belief in me has given me the confidence to endure, to persist, to grow, take risks. To make my world bigger and brighter, even as I stumble over the smallest and simplest things.

Everything I am today, everything I strive to be, is a result of my mother's love, passion and wisdom.
I would not still be here if not for my mum.
Without her guidance, I would never have recovered to the degree that I have.

I love you, Mãe, you are the everything to my everything.

Neuroscientists still have much to learn about how the human brain works or doesn't work. How it heals or doesn't heal.
Despite modern advances in medical care, we still understand very little about how best to treat traumatic brain injuries like mine.
What we do know is that seventy-four million people will suffer a Traumatic Brain Injury (TBI) every single year.
There is so much important work to be done to find a cure for TBI, and to provide greater opportunities and better quality of life for those living with it.

It is for this reason that BTG and I are proud to donate 10 per cent of our royalties from the sale of *Broken Girl* to Brain Injury Australia (BIA).

If reading my story has moved you, and you wish to make a difference, I humbly invite you to join us in supporting BIA's vital medical research, resource centre and public advocacy by making a tax-deductible donation via their official website.

Thank you! Obrigada!

Caroline

THE VOICE OF BRAIN INJURY
brain injury AUSTRALIA
braininjuryaustralia.org.au

Bradley Trevor Greive AM (Yáa Gí Yéil) was born in Tasmania and served in the Australian Army as a paratroop commander. He became a global publishing sensation after the release of *The Blue Day Book* in 2000 and has since sold more than 30 million books in 115 countries, including the internationally bestselling *Penguin Bloom*, and produced numerous films and television programs. In 2014 he was awarded the Order of Australia for his service to literature and wildlife conservation. BTG is a dual Australian-American citizen and a formally adopted member of the Native American Tlingit people of Southeast Alaska. He lives in the USA with his wife, Amy (Jaa.auwdo.laat), daughter, Genevieve (Kaasaandoo.oo), and son, Barrett (Kaa jaax daa keen.aa). Instagram: @tasmanian_grizzly

Caroline Laner Breure was born in Brazil and is a graduate of the Federal University of Rio Grande do Sul and the University of Technology, Sydney. A supply chain professional and vegan entrepreneur, she is the founder and creative director of No Saints (nosaints.co), a boutique sneaker company committed to ethical fashion whose motto is 'Unf*ck the World'. Caroline is still recovering from a traumatic brain injury after being hit by a speeding police car in 2019. A dual Australian-Brazilian citizen, Caroline and her cat, Sundy, are currently based in Portugal. Instagram: @caroline.breure

hachette
AUSTRALIA

If you would like to find out more about Hachette Australia,
our authors, upcoming events and new releases you can visit our
website or our social media channels:

hachette.com.au
HachetteAustralia
HachetteAus

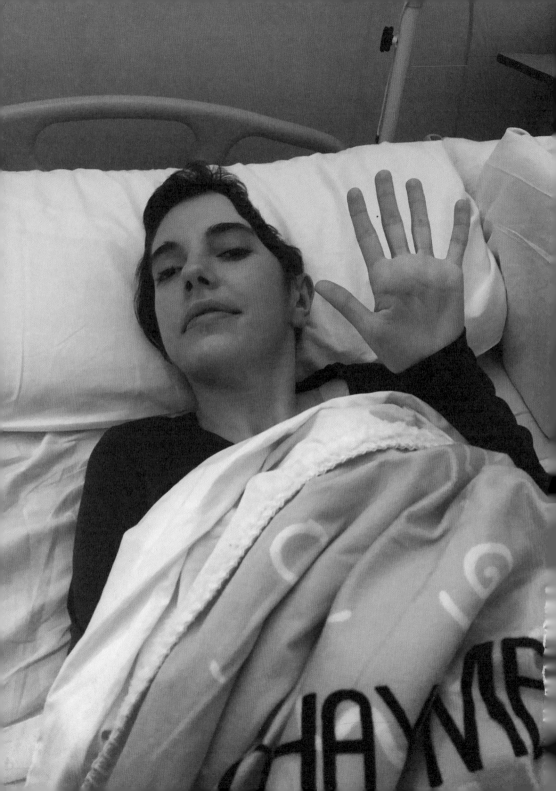